Presented to

_____

From

_____

Date

_____

*God's Word is more
precious than gold...
and sweeter than honey*

Gold & Honey
Bible

BY MELODY CARLSON

ILLUSTRATIONS BY DENNIS OCHSNER

GOLD 'N' HONEY BOOKS • SISTERS, OREGON

Gold & Honey Bible

published by Gold 'n' Honey Books

a division of Multnomah Publishers, Inc.

© 1997 by Multnomah Publishers, Inc.

International Standard Book Number: 1-57673-179-0

Illustrations © 1997 by Dennis Ochsner

Printed in the United States of America

For information:

Multnomah Publishers, Inc.

Post Office Box 1720

Sisters, Oregon 97759

Library of Congress Cataloging-in-Publication Data

Gold & Honey Bible : [Bible stories] / by Multnomah Publishers, Inc.
      p. ca.
      Summary: Presents over one hundred Scripture passages, representing the stories from
creation to Jesus' second coming in the books from Genesis through Revelation.
      ISBN 1-57673-179-0 (alk. paper)
      1. Bible stories, English. [1. Bible stories.] I. Multnomah Books (Firm) II. Gold 'n'
Honey (Firm)
BS551.2.G57 1997
      220.9'505–dc21   97-17256

            CIP

            AC

97 98 99 00 01 – 10 9 8 7 6 5 4 3 2 1

Contents

Old Testament	Page
Let There Be Light	10
The Sky and Sea	14
And Things Began to Grow	18
Creatures of the Deep	22
Wings to Fly	26
Here Come the Animals!	28
God Makes Man	34
God Makes Woman	38
The Serpent's Lie	40
Cain and Abel	44
Noah Builds a Boat	46
The Great Flood	50
The Tower of Babel	54
Abraham Obeys God	56
Abraham and Isaac	60
Isaac and Rebekah	64
Jacob and Esau	68
Jacob Tricks Esau	72
Jacob's Dream	74
Jacob and Rachel	76
Joseph	78

Old Testament	Page
Joseph in Egypt	82
A Plea for Help	86
Baby Moses	90
Moses Runs Away	94
Plagues, Plagues, and More Plagues	98
Moses Leads His People	104
Food from Heaven	110
Water in the Desert	112
Ten Commandments	114
Twelve Explorers	116
Jericho	122
Gideon	128
Samson	132
Ruth and Naomi	136
Hannah's Prayer	142
Samuel	146
King Saul	150
David	154
David and Goliath	156
David the King	160
Solomon	164

Old Testament	Page
Elijah	168
The Widow at Zarephath	170
A Fiery Test	174
Elijah and Elisha	176
Elisha Helps Naaman	178
Queen Esther	182
The Fiery Furnace	190
Daniel and the Lions	194
Jonah and the Big Fish	198

New Testament	Page
An Angel's Visit	204
Mary Visits Elizabeth	206
Joseph's Dream	208
To Bethlehem	210
Born in a Stable	212
The Shepherds' Surprise!	214
Wise Men from the East	216
Jesus Visits His Father's House	222
Jesus is Baptized	226
Tempted in the Wilderness	230
"Come Follow Me"	234
Jesus' First Miracle	240

New Testament	Page
Mountaintop Teaching	244
Things to Remember	248
The Story of the Seeds	252
Two Builders	256
"Love Your Enemies"	260
The Good Fruit Tree	262
The Centurion's Faith	264
The Mustard Seed	268
A Priceless Treasure	270
A Frightening Storm	272
The Woman at the Well	278
Feeding the Crowds	282
He Walks on Water!	286
A Good Neighbor	290
The Greatest in God's Kingdom	296
A Servant's Heart	298
Mary and Martha	300
A Rich Fool	304
The Big Party	308
A Lost Lamb	312
The Blind Man	316
Zacchaeus the Tax Collector	320
A Widow's Gift	324

New Testament	Page
The Good Shepherd	326
Lazarus, Wake Up!	332
Mary's Gift	340
Entering Jerusalem	344
The Servant Of All	348
The Betrayer	352
Jesus Knows	354
The Lord's Supper	358
"Not Me, Lord"	362
My Father's House	364
Like a Vine	366
In the Garden	368
Arrested!	372
Peter Denies Jesus	376
Jesus is Questioned	378
Pilate & Herod	380
The Cross	384
The Darkest Hour	388
He Lives!	390
Thomas Has Doubts	396
A Big Catch of Fish	398
Peter's Second Chance	400
A Job To Do	402

New Testament	Page
Jesus Sends a Helper	404
Rise Up and Walk!	408
Philip Makes a New Friend	412
Saul Sees the Light	416
Paul's Shipwreck Adventure	420
The Holy City	424
Jesus Is Coming Back!	426
Topical Index	429

Foreward

God's Word is alive! The Bible is filled with wisdom and love, faith and adventure, and so much more. We believe a child's first experience with God's Word should be fun and exciting. The Gold & Honey Bible is designed to introduce young hearts to God's awesome power, limitless mercy, and never-ending love.

A children's Bible is like a stepping stone, a way to familiarize a child with God's Word. To that end, we've retold more than one-hundred Bible stories and introduced memorable characters in what we hope is a fresh, new way. We've also been careful to ensure that the Gold & Honey Bible accurately portrays biblical truth, but in an effort to reveal God's larger picture, we have combined or condensed Scripture to make stories more clear and real to children.

Our heartfelt prayer for your child, and for you, is that you will be blessed by God's powerful, living Word, and that it will be planted like a seed and take deep root – to be enjoyed for all eternity!

The Old Testament

Let There Be Light

Genesis 1:1 — 5

*L*ong, long ago, back in the very beginning of time, God created the heavens and the earth. But the earth was blacker than black with darkness. And there was nothing but emptiness both far and wide. Back then, the earth was a lonely place.

Then God said, "Let there be light!"

And then there was light! And God was pleased with the light, for it lit up the whole earth with its sunny brightness and golden warmth.

Now God knew this light was very good, but He did not stop there.

God gently made the earth to spin so that there could also be darkness. He called the dark "night," and the light He called "day."

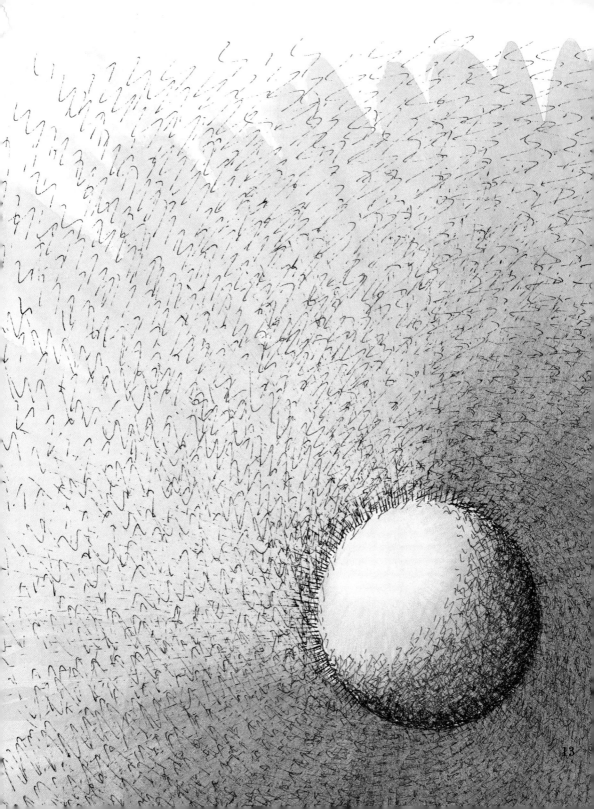

The Sky and Sea
Genesis 1:6—10

God looked upon His earth and said, "Now, let there be sky."

And by the power of His word, He spun layer upon layer of fresh, clean air around the earth, wrapping it in every shade of blue. And He continued until the sky was just right, and the air was perfectly delicious!

15

Then God poured out waters all over the earth. Rushing and gushing, the mighty waters covered the world! He made them flow pure and clean and clear.

Then God divided this gigantic body of water by forming huge mountains and wide valleys, rolling hills, and smooth, flat plains.

The water gathered into clear, sparkling pools and deep blue lakes. And before long, fast-flowing rivers and bubbling streams rushed across the land to greet the mighty oceans.

And Things Began to Grow

Genesis 1:11—13

God made the earth's soil rich and good, and ready to grow. "Let the land produce!" commanded God.

And the earth burst into a garden of life! Plants of all kinds began to spring forth from the warm brown soil. Tender shoots sprouted up from the ground to form fruit trees. Fragile green vegetable seedlings emerged, and soon tightly closed flower buds and blossoms appeared on slender stems.

Soon the fruit trees grew big and strong. Their roots dug deep into the soil, and their branches hung heavy with sweet-smelling fruit. Tall, majestic evergreens stretched toward the sky, reaching their limbs up to heaven.

Luscious green grasses grew, and fragrant flowers bloomed in every color. And their precious seeds were caught by the winds and scattered far and wide. God painted the earth in breathtaking and colorful beauty. And it was so good!

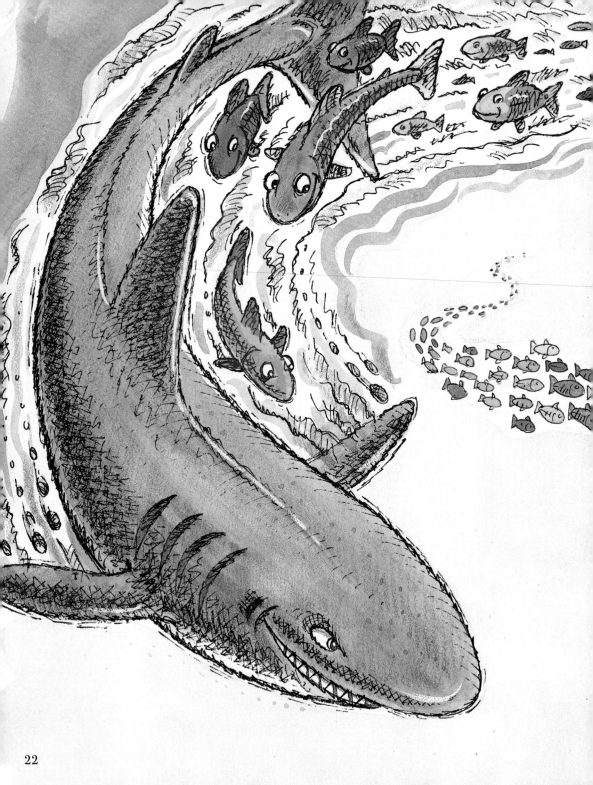

Creatures of the Deep

Genesis 1:20—23

God looked upon the sleeping seas, and by the power of His might, created new life to grow there. He made tiny sea creatures that lived in pretty shells, and funny squids with lots of wiggly legs. He made gigantic whales that could sing in the depths of the sea. And He even created powerful sharks with mouths full of razor-sharp teeth! And to all of these creatures God said, "Now grow and multiply and fill the seas."

And then God filled the fresh waters – the rivers and streams and lakes. He made sleek, silvery fish to swim through the rapids, and bug-eyed frogs with strange, crooked legs. He made turtles with big, hard shells, and funny-looking crawdads with claws to pinch!

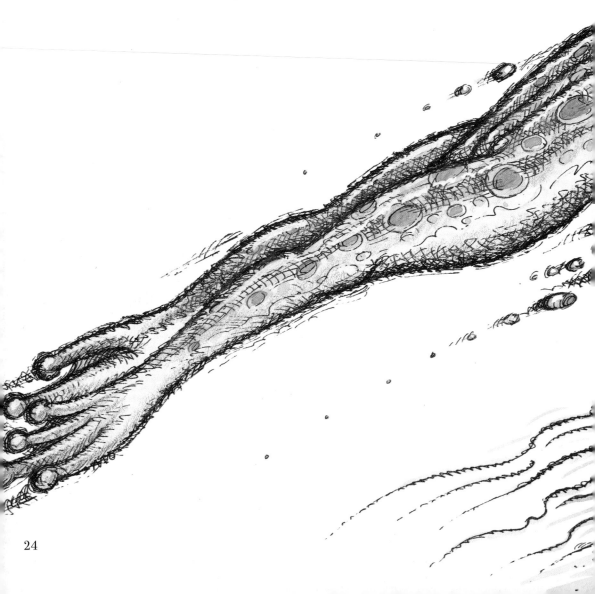

Wings to Fly

Genesis 1:20–23

*L*et birds fill the skies," said God with authority. And it was done!

Bright-colored birds in all sizes and shapes swept across the sky. God made beautiful swans with long, graceful necks, tiny hummingbirds with fast, fluttering wings, and soaring eagles that could speed through the air. Soon the birds' twitters and chirps and peeps filled the land with happy music. And each day they lifted their voices in joyful praise.

Here Come the Animals!

Genesis 1:24—25

*T*he earth was a wonderful place, a beautiful place, a spectacular place. But God had even more ideas!

And so he created all kinds of different animals. He made sleek gazelles that could run like the wind, and elephants with floppy ears and big, strong trunks. He cleverly created the zebras and tigers with dashing stripes; and to the giraffes and leopards, He gave lots of spots. God made big baboons and hairy gorillas to roam in the jungles. And for fun, He made chattering chimps and fun-loving monkeys that could swing and play in the trees!

In other parts of the earth, God made different kinds of animals. In the icy cold regions, He made big polar bears with warm, fuzzy coats, and black-and-white penguins that could slide in the snow.

In the cool forests of the north, God made graceful deer
and majestic elk. He made bears and cougars to roam the
mountains and woods. He made ring-tailed raccoons and
fast-hopping rabbits, frisky squirrels and porcupines with
prickly quills.

In the dry deserts, God made animals that could survive in the sun's bright heat and go without water for long periods of time.

God also made some very special animals that were not wild at all. He made horses and cows, dogs and cats, pigs and goats.

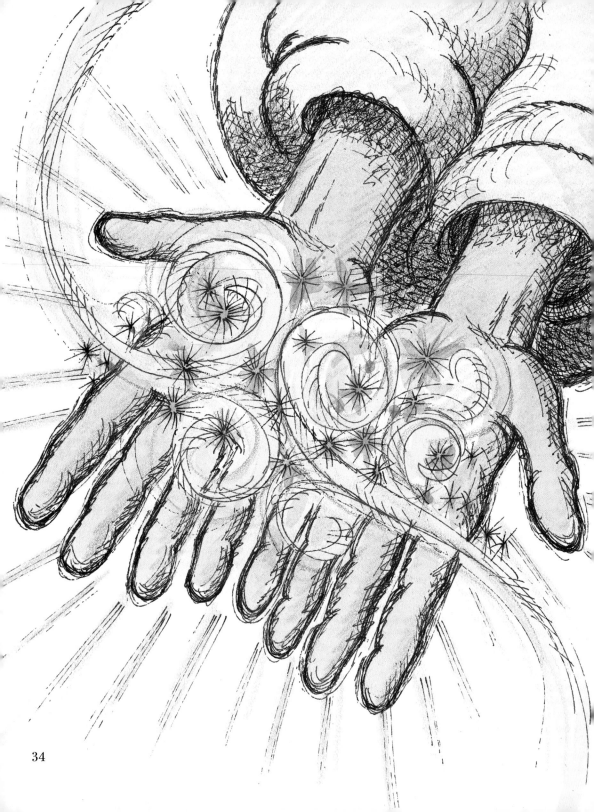

God Makes Man

Genesis 2:7—27

God was very pleased with all that He had made, and it was good. But still it was not enough. God wanted to create someone like Himself. Someone He could walk with and talk with. Someone who could be a friend.

So God scooped up a handful of dust from the earth. Then He gently blew His life into it. And God made man. God named this man Adam, and set him in a very special garden. God had created this beautiful place just for him, and it was called Eden.

God asked Adam to care for the plants and the animals, and to give them names. He told Adam that all the delicious fruits and vegetables in Eden were for him to enjoy – all except for one. God told Adam not to eat from the tree in the center of the garden, because if he did, he would die.

Adam did just as God said, but he had no one to help him. And after a while, Adam became very lonely. The animals had each other, but Adam had no one that was like him.

God Makes Woman

Genesis 2:18—24

God did not want Adam to be lonely, so He made him fall fast asleep. And while Adam slept, God did an amazing thing. He took out one of Adam's ribs and created a woman from it! When Adam awoke, God presented this woman to Adam.

Adam was very pleased with his new friend. And he didn't even mind that God had made her out of his very own bone, because that meant she was like a part of him. Adam named the woman Eve, and they lived very happily in their beautiful garden home.

The Serpent's Lie

Genesis 3

*O*ne day a serpent spoke to Eve. "Did God say you can't eat fruit from any of the trees in the garden?"

"No," explained Eve. "God said we could eat from all of the trees, except for the one in the middle. If we touch that tree, we will die."

"Surely you won't die," hissed the sly serpent. "It's just that God knows if you eat that sweet fruit, you will become as smart as He is."

Eve looked longingly at the ripe fruit. It seemed almost ready to drop into her hand. And it did look delicious. Then she plucked a piece from the tree and ate it.

Eve shared some of the fruit with Adam, and he took a bite. Suddenly they both grew embarrassed, realizing they had no clothes on. So they covered themselves with leaves and hid in the bushes. God called out, "Adam, where are you?" Adam told God what they had done, and God was very sad.

God cursed the serpent for tricking Eve. Then He told Adam and Eve to leave the beautiful garden. And from that day on, Adam would work very hard to provide food for his family, and Eve would suffer great pain when giving birth to their babies. And in the end, they both would die.

Cain and Abel

Genesis 4

Adam and Eve had two sons named Cain and Abel. Abel cared for the sheep, and Cain worked the fields.

One day, the two sons brought gifts to God. Abel brought a little lamb, and Cain brought some grain. But when God was pleased with Abel's lamb, Cain grew very jealous and angry.

"Why are you angry, Cain?" asked God. "If you do what is right, you will be blessed." But Cain was too angry to listen. Instead, he took Abel into the field and killed him. God was disappointed with Cain. He told Cain that he could no longer make things grow. From then on, Cain would wander the earth.

Noah Builds a Boat

Genesis 6

As years passed, more and more people filled the earth. But they no longer listened to God. Instead, they spent every hour of every day thinking up ways to hurt and destroy, ways to cheat and to steal.

God grew very sad as He looked upon His people. Each time they lied or killed or hurt one another, His heart would fill with pain, until one day God was sorry that He had even made them. Finally, God said, "I will get rid of mankind entirely. In fact, I will remove all that moves and breathes from the face of the earth—man and animals and birds."

But before God wiped the entire earth clean, He thought about His good friend, Noah.

Noah had always done what was right, and he had always listened to God. And not only did Noah listen to God, but he always did whatever God told him!

So God told Noah to build an enormous ark—a gigantic boat! It would be bigger than anything that had ever been built before. Noah listened carefully as God explained, step by step, how to make this ark.

Noah and his sons, Shem, Ham, and Japheth, gathered everything they needed and began to build.

The Great Flood

Genesis 6—9

*I*t took a long, long time, but finally Noah and his sons, Shem, Ham, and Japheth, finished building the ark. Then God told Noah to load a male and female of each kind of animal onto the ark. God also told Noah to gather food for all the animals, and for his family, too. Enough for many, many days. That was a lot of food! Finally the ark was loaded.

And then it began to rain. And rain . . . and rain! For forty long days it rained. It was as if all of God's sorrow was pouring down in raindrop tears. Soon the flood water began to swallow the ground, the trees, and even the hills. And as the waters rose, the ark began to float!

Every living thing was wiped from the earth. All except for Noah and his family and the animals on the ark. They floated on the flood waters for more than one hundred and fifty days! Finally God began to dry the land. And before long, the ark came to rest on a mountain.

But still Noah waited and waited. And slowly the waters went down. And finally, God said, "Come out!"

Noah and his family and all the animals spilled from the ark, rejoicing and thanking God. And when they looked up, they saw that God had put a promise across the sky—a rainbow! God said, "Never again will I destroy the earth."

The Tower of Babel

Genesis 11

*A*fter the flood, people filled the earth again. And they all spoke the same language and could talk to each other.

They wanted to build a gigantic tower that could reach all the way to heaven. This tower would make them feel very important. But God said, "If speaking the same language makes them think they can build a tower to heaven, then I will give them all different languages." And He did. Now when they spoke, strange words came out! They could no longer understand each other. And so they could no longer build their tower up to heaven.

Abraham Obeys God

One day, a man named Abraham was told by God, "Abraham, I want you to leave your homeland and everyone you know. Go to a certain place–I will show you how to get there. And when you get there, I will bless you and make you into a great nation."

So Abraham took his wife Sarah and his nephew Lot, and they set out toward the land of Canaan. They brought all their household servants, all their animals, and all their belongings.

Abraham and his household traveled wherever God told them to go. During that time God took very good care of them. But Abraham and Sarah were growing older, and still they had no children. How could God make a man with no children into a great nation?

But one night God said, "Abraham, look up at the heavens and count the stars if you can. That is how many descendants you will have in the years to come."

In time, Abraham and Sarah did have a son, and they called him Isaac. And they thanked God for their beautiful baby boy.

Abraham and Isaac

Genesis 22

*I*saac grew into a strong and healthy boy, and Abraham loved his son with all of his heart—and then some!

One day, God called out, "Abraham!"

"Here I am," said Abraham.

"Abraham, I want you to take your only son Isaac—the one you love so dearly—up to the mountains, and there offer him to Me," said God. "I will show you where to go." Abraham felt sad. He had waited so long for a son, and he didn't want to give him away. But Abraham obeyed.

Early the next morning, he rose and took his only son— the one he loved so dearly—up into the mountains.

After three days, Abraham finally reached the place God had told him about. "Father," said Isaac, "we have fire and wood, but where is the lamb for our offering?"

"God will provide," said Abraham, with tears in his eyes. And he began to carefully arrange the firewood on the altar. At last he bound Isaac and laid him on top.

"Stop!" cried a voice from heaven. "Do not harm the boy. Now I know that you trust Me completely."

Then Abraham saw a ram caught in a thicket. He and Isaac offered the ram to God. And Abraham named the mountain "God will provide."

Isaac and Rebekah

Genesis 24

One day, Abraham said to his servant, "Promise me you will return to my home land to find a good wife for Isaac."

"Shouldn't Isaac come along to pick out his bride?"

"No, Isaac must not go," said Abraham. "God has promised to increase my family. God will help you."

So the servant took ten camels loaded with many gifts, and traveled to Abraham's homeland. When he arrived, he and the camels were very thirsty. He stopped by a spring and prayed, "God, please help me find a good wife for Isaac. When I ask a girl for a drink, let her offer to get water for all of my camels also."

Soon a beautiful girl named Rebekah came and filled her jar with water.

"Please, may I have a drink?" the servant asked.

"Certainly," she said with a smile. "And when you're done, let me also draw water for your camels." She worked hard, and then invited him to stay at her father's home. The servant told her family about Abraham and Isaac, and how he had prayed for God to show him the right woman for Isaac's wife. Rebekah's family loved her dearly, but they believed the servant. They asked Rebekah if she wanted to return with the servant to become Isaac's wife.

Rebekah said, "Yes!"

Jacob and Esau

Genesis 25

*I*saac and Rebekah were married. And Isaac loved his new wife, but for many years they had no children.

Finally, Isaac asked God to give Rebekah a baby. God answered Isaac's prayer and Rebekah became pregnant, but before her baby was born she grew concerned and asked God what was wrong. "Two nations are within you," said God. "The older will serve the younger." Then Rebekah had twins. The first was named Esau and the second, Jacob.

As the boys grew older, Esau became a skilled hunter who loved to spend time outdoors. But Jacob was quieter; he preferred to stay close to home.

One evening, Jacob made stew. Esau came home and said, "Hurry up, give me some of your stew. I'm starving!"

"I'll trade you some stew for your birthright," said Jacob as he stirred the pot. "Then I'll be like the oldest."

"Fine!" said Esau. "My birthright is worthless if I die from hunger!" So Esau gave Jacob his birthright.

Years later, Isaac grew old and weak and blind. He knew he would soon die, so he called to Esau and said, "Go hunt me some wild game, then come and prepare me a tasty meal. After that I will give you my blessing."

Rebekah heard Isaac and grew concerned. Jacob was her favorite son, and she wanted him to have Isaac's blessing.

Jacob Tricks Esau

Genesis 27—28

Rebekah called Jacob and told him her idea. "Hurry and bring me two goats; I'll prepare your father's favorite meal. Then you can serve it to him and get Esau's blessing."

"But he'll know I'm not Esau," said Jacob. "Esau is hairy; my skin is smooth." So Rebekah wrapped goatskins on Jacob's arms, and Jacob set the meal before Isaac. When Isaac finished eating, he gave Jacob the blessing.

When Esau discovered that Jacob had tricked him, he yelled so loud that the walls of the tent shook! He wanted to kill his brother! Rebekah begged Isaac to send Jacob to her family. Isaac agreed. But Esau was still very angry.

Jacob's Dream

Genesis 28

*J*acob left quickly, traveling all day. When night came, he fell asleep under the stars, using a stone for a pillow. As he slept, he had a dream about a beautiful stairway that reached all the way from earth up to heaven! Angels came up and down the stairs, and God said, "I am the God of your fathers, and I will give you and your children the land that you lie upon. All people will be blessed by you. I am with you, and will go with you. And I will do all that I have promised."

Jacob woke up and said, "Surely God is in this place." And he made a vow to God. Then he took the stone he had slept on and set it upright to remember this special place.

Jacob and Rachel

Genesis 29—30

*J*acob arrived at his mother's home-town and asked about his relatives. A man said, "That's your relative, Rachel." So Jacob introduced himself to her and went to meet her father, Laban. In time, Jacob asked to marry Rachel. Laban agreed, but first Jacob must work for seven years! Jacob loved Rachel, so he worked hard. But when the wedding day came, Laban tricked Jacob, giving his older daughter as Jacob's bride. "What have you done?" cried Jacob.

"The oldest daughter always marries first," said Laban, with a sly smile. And so Jacob worked seven more years until he could finally marry Rachel.

Joseph

G e n e s i s   3 7

After many long years of waiting, Jacob and Rachel finally had a baby. It was a day of great rejoicing, and they named this son Joseph. Jacob had eleven other sons, but Joseph was his favorite son. So he made Joseph a beautiful coat with all the colors of the rainbow woven into it. One night, Joseph had an unusual dream. The next day, he told his brothers, "I dreamed we were bundling up wheat. Suddenly, my bundle of wheat rose high in the air, and all of your bundles bowed down before it."

"So you must think you're better than we are!" scolded his brothers. "Shall we bow down to you now?"

One day, Jacob sent Joseph to check on his brothers. They were far off, tending flocks of sheep, but they spotted him walking in the distance. "Here comes the dreamer," they said. "Let's kill him!" And they began to plot against him.

"No, don't kill him," said the oldest. "Just throw him into this hole." When Joseph arrived, they jumped on him, ripped off his beautiful coat, and threw him down into a deep hole. Then they sat and ate their lunch. When a band of merchants passed by, the brothers sold Joseph as a slave. They wiped animal blood on Joseph's coat and took it to their father, telling him that Joseph was dead.

Joseph in Egypt

Genesis 39—41

Joseph was taken to Egypt and sold to a man named Potiphar. Joseph worked hard, and soon Potiphar put him in charge of his entire household. But Potiphar's wife was not a good woman, and one day she accused Joseph of betraying her husband. Although her words were false, Joseph was put in prison. But even in prison, he obeyed God. Joseph liked helping people. Soon he was released to help Pharaoh, the leader of all of Egypt.

"Joseph, I've heard you are able to explain dreams," said Pharaoh.

"Only with God's help," replied Joseph.

God showed Joseph what Pharaoh's dreams meant. Joseph said, "God is warning you. After seven years with plenty of food, the rains will stop. Nothing will grow for the next seven years. But if you plan, you can save your people from starving. You must store food during the good years. Then you can feed your people during the bad years."

"You are a wise man, Joseph," said Pharaoh. "You shall be in charge of all this." Joseph worked hard to carry out the plans that God showed him. He made sure that huge amounts of grain were stored. And when the bad years came, Egypt had plenty of food to feed its people.

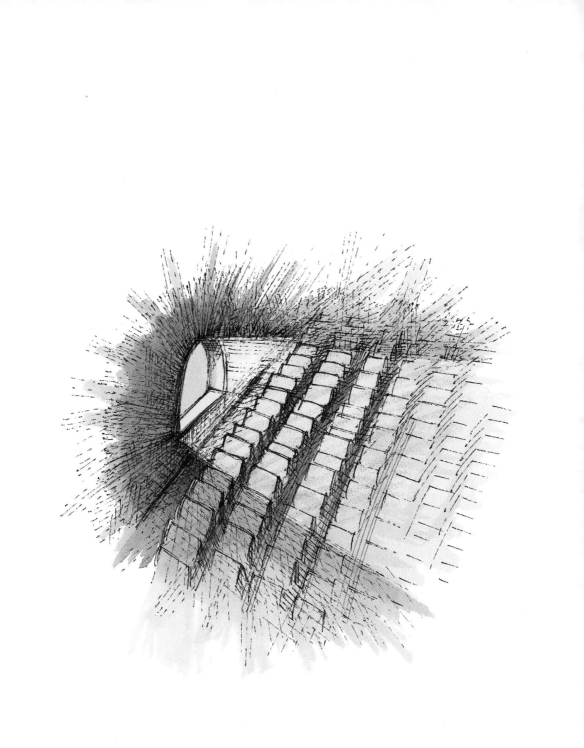

A Plea for Help

Genesis 42—46

*P*eople from all over came to Egypt for food. Even Joseph's brothers came to buy grain. They bowed before the Egyptian governor–not knowing he was Joseph!

"We are the twelve sons of Jacob," they said. "But one brother is dead, and our youngest brother, Benjamin, is at home."

"I think you are spies," said Joseph. "But if what you say is true, then send for this other brother."

They were frightened. Was God punishing them for selling Joseph as a slave? Finally, Joseph allowed them to return to their homeland with food. But he kept one brother, and made them promise to return with Benjamin.

When he heard his sons' story, Jacob sadly agreed to let Benjamin go to Egypt. This time, Joseph invited the brothers into his home, but Joseph still didn't say who he was. Before they left, he hid a silver cup in their things. Then he sent his servant after them. "You've stolen my master's cup!" said the servant. "Now Benjamin must return to Egypt!"

"Please don't take him!" they cried. "Our father lost his son Joseph. It would kill him to lose Benjamin too."

At last Joseph cried out. "I am Joseph! God spared me so I could help you." He sent the brothers back home to get their father. Then he gave them a fine piece of land.

Baby Moses

*M*any, many years later, the Israelites still lived in Egypt. A new Egyptian pharaoh had made them into slaves, but the number of Israelites continued to grow. So the evil pharaoh ordered that all Israelite baby boys be thrown into the Nile River!

One Hebrew mother could not bear to drown her beautiful baby boy. So she wove a sturdy basket in the shape of a tiny boat, and covered the outside with pitch and tar to make it watertight. Then she kissed her baby and set his basket afloat in the reeds along the Nile River. This was where Pharaoh's daughter bathed each day.

Later that day, the princess heard the baby's cries in the reeds. "Bring me that basket," she said to her handmaidens. The baby's sister, Miriam, waited nearby. "Poor little thing," said the princess. "He must be a Hebrew baby."

"Shall I fetch a Hebrew woman to care for him?" asked Miriam hopefully. The princess agreed, and Miriam ran home and got her mother. The baby boy was spared! And his very own mother took care of him.

"I shall name him Moses," said the princess, "for I took him up out of the water." And she raised him as her very own son.

Moses Runs Away

Exodus 2-3

When Moses was a man, he saw an Egyptian beating a Hebrew slave. So he struck and killed the Egyptian. The next day, Moses saw two Hebrews fighting. "Why do you hurt your brother?" he asked.

"Why do you judge us?" demanded one of the men. "Didn't you just kill a fellow Egyptian?" Moses realized that his secret was out, so he ran to hide in a region called Midian. And there he became a shepherd. One day, as he tended sheep in a lonely place, he saw a bush that was on fire. But even though the flames leaped high, the bush didn't burn up. Moses drew closer to examine this strange sight.

"Moses! Moses!" called God. "Stay right there, and take off your sandals, for the ground where you stand is holy. I am the God of your people." Moses obeyed. He fell to his knees and hid his face in fear.

"I have seen my people suffering," said God. "I have heard their cries and felt their pain. I have come to deliver them out of Egypt, and into a land that flows with milk and honey. And you, Moses—you will go to Pharaoh. You will lead my people out of Egypt!"

"But who am I?" asked Moses. "Why me?"

"Because I am with you," said God. "Go and tell Pharaoh to set my people free—to let my people go."

Moses obeyed God. He gathered his family and returned to Egypt. Finally, he stood before Pharaoh, with his brother Aaron at his side. God used Moses and Aaron to perform fantastic miracles. But Pharaoh had a cold, hard heart. Pharaoh refused to listen to God.

Plagues, Plagues, and More Plagues

Exodus 4—12

A while later, Moses met Pharaoh along the banks of the Nile River. "Because you will not listen to God and let His people go, God will turn your river into blood." And the instant Moses' staff touched the water, it became bright red. Every drop of water turned to blood. Fish died, and the smell was dreadful. But even after seven days of this, Pharaoh still refused to listen.

So God sent another plague. And the river grew thick with frogs. The frogs overflowed the banks and began to cover the ground. Frogs were everywhere! People could not walk without stepping on frogs. Pharaoh begged Moses to send the frogs away. He even promised to let God's people go. But when God got rid of the frogs, Pharaoh broke his promise. Pharaoh thought he could trick God.

And so God sent more plagues. Next there were huge swarms of gnats! Then millions of flies! And once again Pharaoh promised to let God's people go. But when the pests were gone, Pharaoh said, "NO!" Then the Egyptian animals died. Yet Pharaoh still refused. Next, the Egyptians became covered in horrible, itching sores, but still Pharaoh said, "NO!" Then God sent locusts, and hail, and even three days of pitch-black darkness. But Pharaoh's heart remained harder than a rock.

Finally, God told Moses, "I will send one last plague. To protect my people, you must mark your homes with lamb's blood. When I pass over Egypt, I will spare the homes with this mark. But all firstborn sons in the unmarked homes will die." God did as He said. Wailing and crying were heard throughout the night. Many Egyptians died, including Pharaoh's own son. But the Israelites were spared. At last, Pharaoh gave up. He called Moses before him.

"GO!" he shouted. "Take your people and leave!"

Moses Leads His People

Exodus 12—15

*I*t was the middle of the night when Moses led the Israelites out of Egypt. There was little time to pack, and no time to gather extra food for the journey. Thousands and thousands of people filed out, leading goats and sheep, and all they could with them.

The Egyptians called out to the Israelites, "Hurry! Hurry! You must leave quickly before we all die!"

As the Hebrews left, Egyptians gave them gold and silver. The Egyptians were weary from the plagues, and hoped that God would now have mercy on Egypt.

God led His people as they traveled. In the daytime, He gave a pillar of cloud to follow. At night, He gave a pillar of fire. Finally, Moses stopped at the banks of the Red Sea and waited for God.

Meanwhile, back in Egypt, Pharaoh changed his mind once again! He gathered his army, setting out with horses and chariots. He wanted to capture the Israelites.

When the Israelites saw the army in the distance, they grew terrified. "Moses!" they cried. "Did you bring us out to the desert so we could be killed by Pharaoh?"

"Don't be afraid," said Moses. "Stand firm! Watch and see what God is able to do!"

Then Moses reached out his hand over the Red Sea. And with great power, God pushed aside the waters, and blew a mighty wind that divided the sea in half! Mothers and fathers, boys and girls, young and old—all walked straight into the sea. But each step they took landed upon dry ground! And next to them stood tall walls of water—one on each side.

For the entire night they walked through the sea. Their eyes grew wide and their hearts trembled when they realized what God had done for them.

Pharaoh's army entered the parted sea, the same as the Israelites had done. But God made the chariots break down and the horses stumble. Meanwhile, the Israelites got safely to shore. Then as the morning sun rose, God told Moses to reach his hand over the sea again. Moses obeyed. And the walls of water immediately fell, thundering back into the sea!

As the Israelites watched Pharaoh's army being buried by the Red Sea, they knew their God was very powerful. They trusted Him. And they trusted Moses–the man God sent to deliver them.

Food from Heaven

Exodus 16

After crossing the Red Sea, the Israelites entered the desert. But God took care of them and watched out for them. Still, it wasn't long before they forgot about God, and began to grumble. "We were better off in Egypt," they complained. "We had good food there."

Then God told Moses He would drop food from the sky— just like rain! "Tell everyone to gather bread each morning, and meat each evening," said God.

The next morning, the ground was coated with white flakes of bread that tasted as sweet as honey. They called it manna. In the evening, quail covered the ground for their meat. God sent them this food the whole time they were in the wilderness.

Water in the Desert

Exodus 17

Moses continued to lead the Israelites through the desert. And once again they began to grumble. "Moses, why did you bring us out here?" they demanded. "It's too hot! Do you want us to die of thirst?"

Moses cried out to God, "What will I do about these people?" Then God told Moses what to do.

Moses did as God said—he chose some older leaders to go with him, and they walked until they reached a certain rock. When Moses struck the rock with his staff, fresh, cool water gushed out—just like a fountain! And once again the people were happy.

Ten Commandments

Exodus 19—20

One day, God called Moses to the top of Mount Sinai. And there He gave Moses a set of ten rules for God's people to live by.

I alone am God; worship no one but Me.

Do not worship things.

Say My name only when you want Me to listen.

Set aside one day each week to rest.

Respect your parents.

Do not take a human life.

Do not break a marriage vow.

Do not steal.

Do not lie.

Do not envy what is not yours.

Twelve Explorers

Numbers 13—14

God said to Moses, "Choose a man from each tribe of Israel, then send them to explore the land of Canaan. For I will give you this land." So Moses picked twelve men, and they set off.

They soon discovered Canaan was a land flowing with milk and honey! It was much better than the desert wilderness they had been traveling through for many years. The men found many delicious fruits to bring back. It took two men just to carry one gigantic cluster of grapes!

After forty days, the explorers returned to report on Canaan. "It's a great place!" some said. "There's lots of food. But the people who live there are powerful, and their cities are huge, with strong walls all around–"

"Wait!" cried an explorer named Caleb. "You're getting it all wrong! God has already promised to give us Canaan. We just need to go in and get what is ours." But already the Israelites were grumbling again.

An explorer named Joshua cried out, "Listen to Caleb! That land flows with milk and honey. God wants us to have it and He will give it to us. Just have faith!"

119

But it was too late. The Israelites were angry and refused to listen. Instead they complained, "It was better in Egypt. Maybe we should go back there."

God was sad when He saw how they turned against Him after all the miracles He had done. Why would they doubt Him now? Where was their faith?

"I will forgive them," God told Moses. "But no one who doubted will set one foot into Canaan."

When Moses told the people what God had said, they were sorry. They started to walk toward Canaan, thinking that they could still have that land. "It's too late now," warned Moses. "God gave you your chance and you doubted Him. If you go to Canaan, you will die."

Jericho

J o s h u a   1 — 6

After many years, Moses died. And God said to Joshua, "Lead My people across the Jordan River. Each place you set your foot will be yours. Just be strong and do not fear. For I am with you wherever you go."

So Joshua sent two men ahead to spy on a town called Jericho. When they got there, they stayed with a woman named Rahab. But when the king of Jericho heard they were spies, Rahab hid them on her roof. And when it grew dark, she helped them to escape.

"I have heard great things about your God," explained Rahab. "Please promise me that you will not hurt my family when your people take Jericho."

God told Joshua exactly what to do in order to take the city of Jericho. First, Joshua gathered men into an army to march around the city. Then came seven priests, each one carrying a trumpet made from a ram's horn. Behind the priests came the ark of the covenant, and following the ark came more armed guards.

They paraded around the city of Jericho one time each day for six days. During this time, the priests blew on the trumpets, but everyone else marched quietly.

On the seventh day, the Israelites paraded around Jericho six times. All the while, the priests blew their trumpets, but everyone else remained quiet.

Then on the seventh time around the city, Joshua called out a signal. Everyone yelled and screamed and shouted—with all their might!

At the sound of that noise, the walls of Jericho began to crumble and then they fell, tumbling to the ground. And all who were inside the city ran in fear. All except for the woman Rahab—the one who had helped the two spies. She knew she would be safe. And she was.

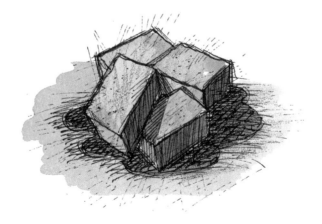

Gideon

Long after the battle of Jericho, the Israelites forgot to obey God again. They hid out in the hills, fearing a people called Midianites. One day, a man named Gideon heard an angel say, "God is with you, mighty warrior!"

"God is with me?" asked Gideon in surprise. "Then why are we having such troubles?"

"You shall save Israel," said the angel. "For God has chosen you to lead your people."

"Me?" cried Gideon. "But who will listen to me? I am no one! I am the least of the least."

"God will go with you," said the angel.

Thousands of men came to help Gideon. But God said, "That's too many. Send back any who are afraid." So Gideon let 22,000 men leave. Now 10,000 remained.

"You still have too many," said God, and He showed Gideon whom to send home. Now only 300 men remained! God told Gideon's army to surround the Midianite camp. When Gideon gave the signal, they smashed jars, waved torches, yelled loudly, and blew their trumpets. The startled Midianites grabbed their swords and fought against themselves. Then they ran! God used Gideon's tiny army to win the battle!

Samson

Gideon lived a good long life, leading Israel. But after he died, Israel forgot to obey God. Soon they were captured by the Philistines, a people who hated God. One day, an angel appeared to an Israelite woman, telling her she would have a son who would save Israel from the Philistines.

When the woman's son was born, she named him Samson. And he grew up to be the strongest man ever!

For years, Samson battled the Philistines. One time, he was attacked by them. Before the fight ended Samson killed 1,000 Philistines with the jawbone of a donkey!

Samson loved a woman named Delilah. He didn't know the Philistines had offered her money to trick him. "Why are you so strong, Samson?" she asked. And although she begged, Samson wouldn't tell. Finally, she cried, "You don't love me, Samson, or you would share your secret."

"It's my vow to God," he whispered. "If my hair is cut, my strength will go." When he fell asleep, she called the Philistines, who paid her and cut his hair. Samson's strength was gone. The Philistines bound and blinded him. Later they threw a big party. But Samson prayed. And God gave him strength to push and collapse their temple. That day, thousands of Philistines died–along with Samson.

Ruth and Naomi

R u t h

A kind, old woman named Naomi lived far from her homeland. Her husband and sons had died. All she had left were her two daughters-in-law. One day, Naomi told them, "I must return to my homeland. I'll miss you, but I'm just an old woman. There's nothing I can do for you."

"Please, Naomi," begged Ruth, one of the daughters-in-law. "Let me go where you go. Your people will be my people. And your God will be my God." And so Naomi agreed. And the two women traveled for many days until they finally reached Naomi's hometown, a place called Bethlehem.

"It's time for the barley harvest, Naomi," said Ruth. "If I gather leftover grain, we can make bread to eat." So Ruth got permission to pick up grain missed by the harvesters.

A man named Boaz owned the field and wondered who she was. "She came back with old Naomi," said his foreman. "All day long, she has worked hard."

Boaz called Ruth to him and said, "Gather as much grain as you need, and my workers will watch for you."

"You are very kind to a foreigner," she said.

"You helped my relative Naomi," said Boaz. "May God bless and reward you for your kindness."

God did bless Ruth. In time she and Boaz became friends. Boaz shared food, and helped her whenever he could.

One night, Naomi told Ruth to go to the threshing floor where Boaz was sleeping. She told Ruth to wait for him there. When Boaz awoke he was surprised to see Ruth. "What are you doing here?" he asked.

"Naomi has sent me," said Ruth. "Since you are her nearest relative, I have come to ask you to care for us."

"God bless you," said Boaz. "And don't be afraid, for I will take care of you."

Naomi rejoiced when Ruth and Boaz got married. And Ruth became the great-grandmother of the great King David!

Hannah's Prayer

1 Samuel 1

*H*annah was a good woman who loved God. But she was sad, for she had no children. Each year, her husband took her to a place called Shiloh, where they worshiped God. And each year, Hannah prayed a special prayer that God would give her a child. One year, she prayed, "Dear God, if You will only give me a son, I will give him back to You, to serve You all his days." She prayed so hard her mouth moved, but no words came out. A priest asked if she was drunk. "No," she said. "I'm pouring my heart out to God."

"May you find favor in God's eyes," said the priest.

The following year, Hannah couldn't make the trip to Shiloh with her husband because God had answered her prayers. She had a new baby boy named Samuel!

She happily cared for Samuel until he was old enough to leave her. Then she kept her promise to God, and took Samuel to live with the priests in Shiloh. It wasn't easy for her to say good-bye, but each year she made him a special robe to wear as he served God.

God gave Hannah many more children. And Hannah was pleased to know that Samuel was growing up in Shiloh, where he would love and serve God always.

Samuel

1 Samuel 3,8

*O*ne night, when Samuel was a boy, he heard a voice calling. He thought it was the old priest Eli, but Eli said, "I didn't call you; go back and lie down." Samuel heard the call again, but Eli still said it wasn't him. When Samuel heard it for the third time, Eli said, "It must be God. Go back and listen." So Samuel went back, and God spoke.

But Samuel didn't want to tell Eli what God had said, because God was very unhappy with Eli's sons.

"Do not hide God's words from me," said Eli. And so Samuel told Eli, and Eli listened. From then on Samuel always said what God told him to say.

Samuel continued to serve God. All of Israel knew that Samuel was a man they could trust to speak God's words. Even when they went through hard times, Samuel reminded them of God's words. People all over Israel respected Samuel. And for a while, Israel lived in peace. Samuel helped them to remember to listen to God.

When Samuel grew old, the people of Israel said they wanted a king. Samuel felt bad and told God of this, and God said, "They aren't rejecting you, Samuel. They are rejecting Me." For until then, God had been their king.

King Saul

Samuel warned Israel that getting a king would bring problems, but the people would not listen. They wanted to be like all the other countries who had kings.

There was a young man named Saul who was very tall and handsome. One day, he and a servant were out looking for a herd of lost donkeys that his father owned. They went for miles and miles, and finally Saul wanted to go back home. But the servant said, "There is a prophet in this town. Maybe he can tell us where the donkeys are." So Saul and the servant went to see Samuel.

God had told Samuel the day before that a stranger would come to town—the man chosen by God to rule Israel. Samuel met Saul and said, "I am the one you're looking for. Your donkeys have been found. Now God wants to bless you and your family." Then Samuel invited Saul to an important dinner. He seated Saul at the head of the table.

The next morning, Samuel poured oil on Saul's head and said, "God has chosen you to lead his people. God's spirit will come upon you, and God will help you to rule his people." After Saul left, all that Samuel said took place. And Saul became the first king of Israel.

David

1 Samuel 16

After King Saul disobeyed God, God told Samuel to find a new king. This time, God showed Samuel a boy named David who tended sheep for his father. God said, "I don't look at the outside of a person, I look at the heart." So Samuel poured oil on David's head to show that he would be the next king of Israel.

Later on, when King Saul couldn't sleep at night, he asked for a musician to play for him. His servant said, "There is a young man who plays beautiful harp music. He is a brave man who loves God." So David came and played his harp for the king, and Saul was pleased with David and his music.

David and Goliath

1 Samuel 17

One day, David delivered food to his brothers who were battling the Philistines. He heard a Philistine shouting and making fun of them.

"Who is that man?" asked David. They told him about Goliath, the mighty warrior. No one could defeat him! But David wasn't afraid of the giant. When King Saul heard of David's bravery, he called David before him.

"Don't worry, I'll go fight that giant," said David.

"But he's a warrior," said Saul. "You're only a boy."

"I killed a lion and bear to protect my father's sheep," said David. "God will help me kill this giant."

Saul gave David his armor and weapons. But they were too big for David.

So without any armor, David went to face the giant. He stopped by a stream to pick up some stones and placed them in his bag. Then he stood before Goliath.

"Am I a dog that you come at me with sticks?" bellowed Goliath.

David looked up and said, "You come against me with weapons, but I come against you in the name of the Lord Almighty. This is God's battle!" Then David put a stone in his sling and swung it around and around until the sling whistled. The stone whizzed through the air and smacked Goliath right in the forehead. And the giant fell to the ground with a mighty earth-shaking thud!

David the King

2 Samuel 1 - 7

Stories and songs about David's bravery traveled across the land. Soon King Saul became very jealous of him. He even tried to kill David, but God protected David.

When Saul died, David became the new king of Israel. David led the Israelites through many victorious battles against their enemies. Before long, David conquered Jerusalem and it was called the City of David. He built a palace there. Everyone loved King David!

The Israelites rejoiced when David and his men brought the Ark of God into the City of David. And King David danced on the streets, praising God!

With all their enemies defeated, Israel enjoyed a time of peace. David loved God, and his greatest wish was to build a temple for God. But David didn't always obey God. So finally God told David that David's son would be the one to build God's temple.

David wrote many beautiful songs to God. Most were to praise God, but some were to say he was sorry. David loved to worship God with his songs.

Solomon

After a good, long life, King David died. David's son, Solomon, became Israel's king.

One night, God appeared to King Solomon in a dream. "Ask for whatever you want," said God, "and I will give it to you."

"You did so much for my father," said Solomon. "And his kingdom was great, but now that I am king, I feel like a little child. I don't even know how to rule. So please make my heart wise so that I can do what is right for Your people." God was glad that Solomon didn't ask for riches or long life. God granted King Solomon's wish, and Solomon became the wisest man ever. God also gave Solomon a long life and great riches.

Just as God had promised David, Solomon built God's temple. Many, many builders worked for seven years to complete this beautiful building. Skilled craftsman decorated it with carved wood and fine gold.

When it was finished, Solomon held a huge celebration to dedicate the temple. For fourteen days the people worshiped God at the temple! Although the temple was wonderful, Solomon knew that it was not great enough to contain the Almighty God. But God promised Solomon that His eyes and His heart would always be on the temple, and with His people.

Elijah

1 Kings 17

After King Solomon died, many kings ruled Israel, one after the other. Some were good, some were bad. King Ahab was very bad. He turned his back on God.

During King Ahab's time, there was a man called Elijah who listened to God and spoke for God. He was a prophet.

One day, Elijah told King Ahab, "God has shown me there will be no rain for the next few years unless I say so." Then Elijah went off to hide in a place that God showed to him. Each day, God sent ravens to carry meat and bread for Elijah to eat. The birds came in the morning and the evening. And Elijah drank water from the stream.

The Widow at Zarephath

After many days, the water dried up in Elijah's stream. And God told him to go find a widow in a place called Zarephath.

Sure enough, when Elijah arrived, he found a woman gathering sticks.

"Would you bring me a drink of water?" he called to her. She agreed. As she went for water, Elijah added, "And could you bring me a piece of bread also?"

"As sure as God lives, I have none," she said. "I have only a drop of oil and a handful of flour. Right now, I'm taking these sticks home to make a fire. I will cook that last bit of bread for myself and my son. Then we will eat it and die."

"Don't worry," said Elijah. "Go and make your bread. But then bring it to me. After that you can make more for you and your son. For God has told me that your flour will not be used up, and your oil will not run dry. Not until the day that God sends rain to this land."

So the widow went home and did exactly as Elijah said. And he was right! The flour and the oil did not run out. She made bread every single day for many, many days. Her flour and oil lasted until God sent rain.

A Fiery Test

*A*fter three years, God told Elijah to speak to the wicked king.

"Ahab," said Elijah, "you've turned from God, and you serve the false god Baal. Now let's see whose God is real!"

So Ahab's false prophets made an altar with wood piled high. "Can your gods make your wood burn?" asked Elijah. Ahab's false prophets danced and shouted, but their altar did not burn. "Perhaps your gods are asleep," said Elijah. "Or maybe they've taken a trip." Then Elijah made an altar for God. He piled it high with wood, and poured gallons of water on it! Elijah prayed, and the altar burst into fiery flames!

The people cried out, "The Lord God-He is God!"

Elijah and Elisha

1 Kings 19, 2 Kings 2

God chose a man named Elisha to follow Elijah and they became good friends. Elisha served Elijah faithfully. But one day, Elijah said, "Elisha, you stay here. God is sending me away."

"As God lives, I will never leave you," said Elisha, and he continued to stay with Elijah. Each time Elijah told Elisha to say behind, Elisha refused to leave his friend.

"What can I do for you before I go?" asked Elijah.

"I want a double share of your spirit," said Elisha.

Then a chariot of fire swept down from heaven and took Elijah away. But God answered Elisha's request, and like his friend, Elisha became a powerful prophet too.

Elisha Helps Naaman

2 Kings 5

*N*aaman was a good man who commanded an army in the country of Aram. But Naaman had a problem. He had a bad disease called leprosy.

"Naaman should go see the great prophet Elisha," said a Hebrew girl who worked for Naaman's wife. "Elisha could heal Naaman."

So Naaman gathered gifts of silver, gold, and fine clothes, and set off for Israel. When he finally reached Elisha's house, Elisha didn't even come out. Instead he sent a messenger to Naaman. "Go and bathe in the Jordan River seven times," said the servant. "And then you will be healed." But Naaman didn't like this message.

"I could have stayed home and bathed in my own river!" said Naaman. "I expected more from this prophet."

But Naaman's servants convinced him to give it a try. And so he did. When Naaman came out of the water the seventh time, he was completely healed!

Naaman said to Elisha, "Your God is the only true God. Please accept these gifts as my thanks."

"As the Lord lives, I will not," said Elisha. For Elisha did not want to be paid for what God had done. And so Naaman went on his way, but Elisha's servant followed him. The servant lied to Naaman and took Naaman's gifts. But when the servant returned, Elisha knew everything.

"Because of your dishonesty," said Elisha to the servant, "you will now have Naaman's leprosy."

Queen Esther

Esther

*K*ing Xerxes ruled over the mighty land of Persia. When he needed a wife, his servants searched the land for the most beautiful women. They brought these women to the palace so the king could choose his bride. A woman named Esther was chosen. She was good and wise and very beautiful. But she was an Israelite. A kind relative named Mordecai had adopted Esther as a child, and raised her as his own daughter. He warned her not to tell anyone she was an Israelite.

When King Xerxes saw Esther, he was very pleased! He set the royal crown on her head, and she became his wife and queen. Then the king gave a big party to celebrate!

Mordecai often sat by the palace gates to hear how Esther was doing. One time, he overheard men plotting to kill the king. Mordecai warned Esther, and she told the king. The bad men were arrested, and Mordecai's good deed was written in the king's record book.

Later on, a powerful man named Haman became angry at Mordecai. Haman knew that Mordecai was an Israelite, and he encouraged King Xerxes to make it legal to kill all Israelites.

Esther knew this law meant that she too must die. "I will do all I can to change this," she said to Mordecai. " Even if it means that I am killed. Please ask my people to pray for me."

And Mordecai did.

Esther wanted to speak to the king. When King Xerxes saw her, he asked, "What can I do for you, dear Queen? I will give you whatever you ask, up to half my kingdom."

"I have prepared a banquet for you and Haman. I would like you to be my guests," said Esther.

So the king and Haman came and enjoyed a delicious meal served by Esther. "Now, dear Queen, tell me what it is I can do for you," said King Xerxes.

"If you both could come for another feast tomorrow," said Esther, "then I will tell you my request."

The next day, King Xerxes and Haman came to another fine banquet. "Now, tell me, my Queen, what is your request?" said King Xerxes. "What can I give to you?"

"Dear King," said Esther. "If you are pleased with me, I beg you to spare my life. And also spare the lives of my people. If we were to be sold as slaves, I would not have bothered you, but it seems unfair that we are to be put to death."

"Who dares to do this?" demanded the king.

"It is this cruel Haman," said Esther, pointing to her enemy. The king ordered Haman to be hung that very same day.

Esther and her people were safe!

190

The Fiery Furnace

Daniel 3

Many, many years later, Israel was defeated by Babylon. Many Israelites were taken captive and marched off to Babylon.

The king of Babylon's workers had built a giant golden statue. And the king made a law commanding everyone to bow down and worship the statue whenever they heard the king's special music.

But Shadrack, Meshack, and Abednego were Israelites. They refused to worship the statue. They would only worship the one true God.

So the king ordered that these young men be thrown into a huge fiery furnace. But first he said, "Make the fire seven times hotter than usual!"

The king watched as they were thrown into the furnace. "Weren't only three men thrown into the fire?" asked the king. His servants agreed. "But I see four men," he said, "and one of them looks like a god!" The king approached the furnace. "Shadrack, Meshack, Abednego!" he yelled, "servants of the Most High God, come out!"

And so the three came out. Nothing on them was burnt, and they didn't even smell of smoke.

"Your God is great!" cried the king. "He sent His angel to rescue you. From now on, no one will be allowed to say anything bad about your God."

Daniel and the Lions

Daniel 6

Later on, King Darius ruled Babylon.
King Darius respected Daniel. He
knew Daniel was a godly man who had served the kings
before him. But some of King Darius' men did not like
Daniel. They wanted to get rid of him. So they convinced the
king to make a law forbidding people to pray to anyone but
the king. And anyone who broke this law would be thrown
into the lions' den!

Daniel knew about the law, but he continued to pray to
God. The men spied on Daniel, and then told the king that
Daniel had broken the law and must be thrown to the lions!

The king sadly agreed, and Daniel was put into the lions' den.

"May your God rescue you," said the king. That night, the king could not eat or sleep. He was too worried about Daniel.

Early the next morning, he ran out to the lions' den.

"Daniel!" he cried, "has your God been able to rescue you from the hungry lions?"

"King Darius," called Daniel, "may you live forever. Yes, my God sent His angel to shut the lions' mouths! They have not hurt me." Then King Darius had the evil men who'd made the bad law thrown into the lions' den. And this time, God did not close the lions' mouths.

Jonah and the Big Fish

Jonah 1-3

*J*onah," said God, "go to Ninevah and tell them I've seen their wickedness."

But Jonah didn't like the people of Ninevah. And he thought he could run away from God. So he got on a ship sailing away from Ninevah.

Soon a storm began to beat upon the ship until the sailors were afraid that it would break into pieces. The wind roared and the waves crashed!

Finally, Jonah realized he was the reason for the terrible storm. "Throw me overboard," said Jonah, "and the storm will end."

The sailors didn't want to throw Jonah out, but the storm grew even wilder. At last they agreed. They threw Jonah into the sea. Instantly, the sea became calm.

200

Then God sent a gigantic fish to swallow Jonah. For three days and three nights, Jonah stayed inside the fish. While he was inside the fish, he asked God to help him.

Finally, God made the fish spit Jonah out onto dry land. And this time, Jonah obeyed God. He went straight to Ninevah and began to preach.

"God has seen your wickedness," said Jonah. "He will destroy Ninevah in forty days."

The people listened to Jonah. They were sorry for the bad things they had done. They began to pray. They returned to God. And God did not destroy them.

The New Testament

An Angel's Visit

Luke 1

One day, an angel appeared to a young woman named Mary. "God is happy with you," said the angel. "You have been chosen to have a baby boy! You will call him Jesus, and He will be great. He will be the Son of the Most High!"

Mary stared at the angel. "How can this be?" she asked.

"God will send His Holy Spirit to give you this baby," said the angel. "And God has done another miracle. After many years of waiting, God will give your relatives Elizabeth and Zechariah a son. See, nothing is impossible with God."

Mary bowed. "I am God's humble servant. I will do all that you have said." Then the angel left.

Mary Visits Elizabeth

Luke 1

Mary quickly left to go visit Elizabeth. Elizabeth met her at the door with a big smile. "Mary!" Elizabeth cried with joy. "When I heard your voice, the baby inside me leaped! Now I must ask you—why has the mother of my Lord come to see me?"

Mary was amazed that Elizabeth already knew what God was doing. Mary stayed with Elizabeth for several months before she returned to her home.

Joseph's Dream

Matthew 1

*M*ary was engaged to wed a kind man named Joseph. But he was upset. Joseph did not understand why Mary was to have a baby before they were married.

Then one night, an angel appeared to Joseph in a dream. And the angel said, "Joseph, do not be afraid to take Mary as your wife. For God has chosen her, and blessed her to give birth to His very own Son. And this child shall be called Jesus, and He will save His people from sin."

To Bethlehem

Luke 2

*I*n those days, a law was passed that everyone must travel to their hometowns to have their names written down. Although Mary was almost ready to have her baby, she and Joseph had to go to Bethlehem, which was also called the city of David.

After a long, tiring journey, they finally reached the small town. Mary knew it was time for God's Son to be born, and she was very weary from traveling and wanted a place to rest. But many people bustled through the crowded streets–they too had come to record their names. And although Joseph searched the whole town, he could not find a room for them to stay in.

Born in a Stable

Luke 2

At last, Joseph found a shelter for Mary to rest. It was only a stable for oxen, cattle, and donkeys. Not a palace, not a lovely home–and yet, it was exactly the right spot, the very place God had chosen. And before long, Mary gave birth to God's only Son.

Mary wrapped sweet baby Jesus in clean strips of soft cloth. Then she gently laid Him upon the straw in a wooden manger, the very same manger that the oxen and cows had eaten from.

The Shepherds' Surprise!

Luke 2

*N*ot far away, there were shepherds caring for sheep on a hillside. Suddenly a bright light shone, and an angel appeared before them! "Don't be afraid," said the angel. "God has sent me to tell you the greatest news! This very day, a Savior is born in the city of David! You will find him lying in a manger." Then the night burst into brilliant light and beautiful sound as hundreds of angels filled the sky. "Glory to God!" they shouted. "Peace on earth! Good will to all mankind!"

The shepherds left the hillside and quickly went down to Bethlehem. And just as the angels had said, they found baby Jesus lying in a manger.

216

Wise Men from the East

Matthew 2

Some time after Jesus was born, wise men journeyed to Jerusalem. They had carefully studied the stars and learned that a King had been born in that region. They stopped at King Herod's palace. "Where is this newborn King?" asked the wise men. "We have seen His star and know that He is to be King of the Jews. We want to worship Him." But King Herod didn't like this news, for he was the king of the Jews! He did not want to share his throne with anyone. And certainly not with a baby!

King Herod called in priests and scribes. "What do the prophets say about a King like this?" he demanded.

"The Scriptures say a very special King will be born in the town of Bethlehem," explained the learned men. "And He will be a shepherd to God's people."

Then King Herod called back the wise men and told them to seek this King in Bethlehem. "And when you find Him," said King Herod, "you must return and tell me where He is, so I too can worship Him." But the truth was, King Herod did not wish to worship Jesus—he only wanted to kill Him!

The wise men traveled to Bethlehem and found Mary and Joseph and baby Jesus. They worshiped Him and presented valuable gifts of gold, frankincense, and myrrh. God warned the wise men not to return to Herod's palace and tell the evil king about baby Jesus. God also warned Joseph to flee from Bethlehem! King Herod planned to kill all the baby boys born there to get rid of Jesus, the newborn King.

And so Joseph quickly took Mary and Jesus to Egypt, and there they stayed until it was safe to return to their home-land again.

Jesus Visits His Father's House

Luke 2

*J*esus grew. Even when He was still young, He was very wise. And He was kind and good and honest.

When Jesus was twelve, He traveled with His parents, and other friends and relatives, to Jerusalem to celebrate the Passover. When the celebration was finished, the group began their journey back home. But after many miles, Mary and Joseph realized that Jesus was not among the crowd of travelers.

"Jesus, where are You?" cried Mary and Joseph as they searched along the roadside for Jesus. They hurried back to Jerusalem. For three days, they searched without finding Him.

Finally, Mary and Joseph stopped at the temple. And there was Jesus! He was sitting with the teachers, listening and asking them questions. All who heard Jesus speak were astonished at His wisdom. Mary ran up to Him. "Jesus!" she cried. "Why did You do this? Your father and I have been looking all over for You!"

"Didn't you know I would be in My Father's house?" He asked.

Mary and Joseph did not understand exactly what He meant by this, but they all traveled happily back home. And Jesus continued to grow into a man who was loved and respected by both God and men.

Jesus is Baptized

Matthew 3

Many years later, John the Baptist began to preach in the wilderness around Judea. He wore a rough, heavy garment made of camel's hair, and for food he ate grasshoppers and wild honey. "Repent," he cried. "And stop doing wrong! God's Kingdom is coming soon!" People from miles around came to hear John preach. And hundreds prayed, telling God they were sorry for their sin. Then John baptized them in the Jordan River.

"I baptize with water," John explained to the crowds. "But a greater One is coming! He will baptize you with the Holy Spirit–and with fire!" The crowd gasped in wonder. How could someone baptize with fire?

Jesus left Galilee and traveled to the place where John was preaching. He asked John to baptize Him. "I, baptize You?" cried John in disbelief. "I am not fit to carry Your sandals. You should baptize me!"

"Please," said Jesus. "It is right for you to do so." And so John obeyed Jesus, baptizing Him the same way he had baptized others in the Jordan River.

As Jesus rose from the water, the heavens split open with a burst of glorious light! And God's Spirit flew down and landed upon Jesus in the form of a beautiful dove. A voice spoke from heaven. "This is My beloved Son, and I am very, very pleased with Him!"

229

Tempted in the Wilderness

Matthew 4

After His baptism, Jesus spent time alone with God in the wilderness. For forty days, He ate no food. He grew very, very hungry. "Jesus," called a voice, "if You are really God's Son, why don't You turn these stones into bread so that You can eat?"

Jesus recognized Satan's voice, and although He was hungry, He said, "It is written, 'Man does not live by eating only bread, but by every word that comes from God's mouth.'"

Then Satan showed Jesus the peak of the temple and said, "If You are really God's Son, You could jump from here and Scripture says angels would catch You."

"It also says, 'Do not tempt God,'" answered Jesus.

So Satan took Jesus to the top of a tall mountain and said, "Look down there. See all that lies below You, every kingdom, every single thing on the earth. Bow down and worship me, and I will give it all to You."

"Get away from me, Satan!" commanded Jesus. "It is written, 'Worship God alone, and serve only Him.'"

At that, Satan fled, and angels came down and cared for Jesus.

"Come Follow Me"

Mark 1—3

*J*esus knew it was time to return to Galilee. And there, He began to preach. One day, He walked along the sandy shore next to the Sea of Galilee. Many fishermen worked at the water's edge, mending nets, tending boats, and discussing the day's catch. Jesus called out, "Simon and Andrew! Come follow Me, and I will teach you to fish for men." The two brothers instantly left their nets and joined Jesus.

The three walked along until Jesus saw two more fishermen, who were also brothers. "James and John," He called, "come, follow Me." And these men left their boats and went with Jesus.

Jesus saw a man named Levi, who was later called Matthew, working at his tax office. Jesus called out, "Levi, come and follow Me!" And Levi stood up, left the office, and followed Jesus. Later, Jesus went to Levi's house for a meal. But no one liked tax collectors, and the religious leaders questioned why Jesus would eat with someone like Levi and his sinful friends.

But Jesus said, "Healthy people don't need to see a doctor. I came to call sinners, not those who already think they are good."

Then Jesus chose seven more men to follow Him. That gave Him twelve men altogether. They would become His closest friends–His disciples. The names of the twelve were: Simon who was later called Peter, James and John (the sons of the fisherman, Zebedee), Andrew, Philip, Bartholomew, Matthew, Thomas, James (the son of Alphaeus), Thaddaeus, Simon the Zealot, and Judas Iscariot (the one who would one day betray Jesus).

239

Jesus' First Miracle

J o h n 2

*J*esus and His disciples went to a wedding celebration in Cana. Jesus' mother, Mary, was also there. "Jesus," whispered Mary, "there's a problem here. They have run out of wine to serve the wedding guests."

"Why are you telling Me this?" asked Jesus.

Mary just smiled and called the servants over. "Now, do whatever Jesus says," she instructed them.

Jesus then pointed to six large water jugs. "Fill those with water," He said to the worried servants.

The servants filled the jugs with water, then stood before Jesus expectantly. "Now," said Jesus, pointing to a jug, "dip some out and present it to the master of this banquet." The servants did just as Jesus said.

The master tasted it and smiled. He took the bridegroom aside and said, "Usually they serve the finest wine at the beginning of the wedding celebration. But you, you have saved the very best for last!"

Jesus' disciples were amazed by this miracle! Who was this man who cared enough about a wedding party to change ordinary water into wine? And they all decided to put their faith in Him.

Mountaintop Teaching

Matthew 5—6

More and more people began to listen to Jesus. Whenever He spoke, a large crowd usually gathered.

One day, Jesus took His disciples to a quiet mountainside. He sat down and began to teach.

"You are the light of the world!" He said to them. "A city on a hill is hard to hide. And when you light a lamp, do you put a bucket on top of it? No, of course not! You set it on a table so the whole house is lit by it.

"Let your life shine like a bright light so others will praise God the Father for the good He is doing in you!"

Jesus warned them, "Be careful when you help people or give to those in need. Make sure you do it quietly and from your heart. Don't make a big show so people will praise you. God will reward you! And when you pray, don't use fancy words and talk loudly. But pray in a quiet place–God is listening."

Jesus taught them this prayer:

Dear Father in heaven,

Your name is the most holy.

Let Your kingdom rule,

Let Your will be done,

On earth just like in heaven.

Give us what we need for today.

Forgive us when we do wrong,

And help us to forgive others who do wrong.

Lead us far away from what tempts us,

And save us from evil.

Your kingdom and power and glory will last forever!

Amen.

Things to Remember

Y ou don't need to hide away treasures
for yourselves on earth," explained
Jesus. "These things are so easily lost, or stolen, or ruined.
But if your treasure is in heaven, nothing can take it from
you! And remember, the place where you keep your treasure
is the same place where you keep your heart."

Jesus watched as birds flew by, singing sweetly in the air.
"You don't need to worry, or ask what will I eat, what will
I wear? Your life is more important than food and clothes."
Jesus pointed up. "See those birds? They don't plant gardens
or sew clothes. Yet God the Father gives them what they
need. Remember you're more precious to God than birds.
He will take good care of you!"

"Don't look down upon others," said Jesus. "Don't point your finger and blame them, or say mean things about them—unless you want to be treated like that! It's like telling someone he has a speck of sawdust in his eye when you have a great big board sticking in yours. Take care of your own problem before you try to fix someone else's problems."

"Ask," said Jesus, "and you will receive. Seek, and you will find. Knock, and the door will be opened for you! If a child asks his parents for a piece of bread, will his parents give him a rock to eat? Of course not! So think about how much more your Father in heaven loves you. Think about how He longs to give you good gifts."

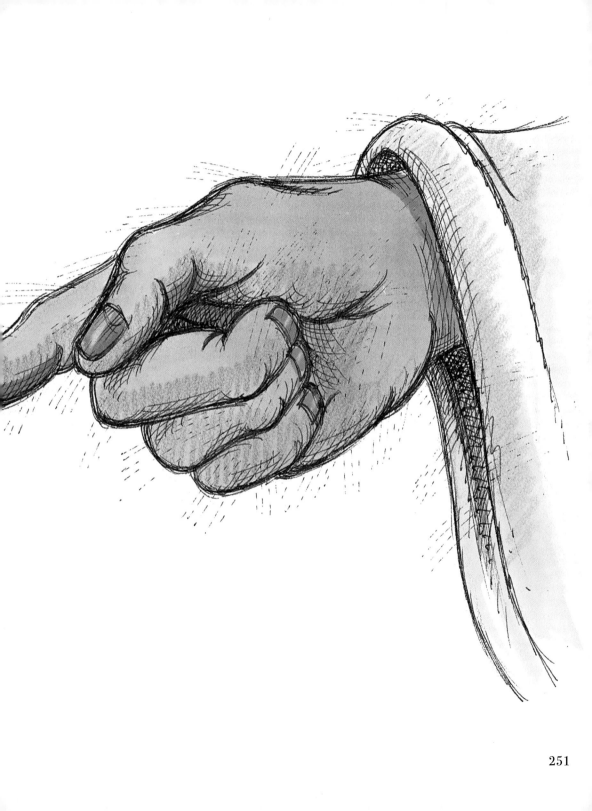

The Story of the Seeds

Mark 4

*H*ere's a story for you," said Jesus. "There once was a farmer who went out to plant seeds. Some of the seeds fell upon the hard-packed footpath, and hungry birds came and gobbled them up. Other seeds fell into a rocky place where there was no good soil for roots, but the plants sprang up anyway–until the sun came out and they withered and died.

"Then some seeds fell among the weeds and they grew, but before long the weeds choked out the good plants so they never produced any grain. And finally some of the seeds were planted into the good, healthy soil. And these plants grew up strong and tall, and produced a good crop."

But the people didn't understand the meaning of the seed story. Later, Jesus explained it to His disciples.

"You see, the seeds are like God's word. Some people hear God's word, but Satan steals it away–just like the hungry birds that ate the seeds right off the path. Other people are like the seeds that sprang up quickly in the rocky soil–they are excited and joyful when they first hear God's word. But their faith isn't deep–they have no roots. When troubles come they have no strength, they're like the plants that withered in the sun.

"And then there are those who hear God's word, but worry about getting rich. Their worries crowd out the truth–the same way the weeds crowded out the good plants."

"But finally," continued Jesus with a smile. "There are those people whose hearts are eager and ready to hear God's word. They are like good healthy soil, and God's word can make deep roots in them. They will grow and God's goodness will be like fruit in their lives."

Two Builders

Luke 6

*J*esus told another story:

"There was once a man who wanted to build a sturdy house. So he dug deep into the earth and made a foundation of solid rock. It was hard work, but he knew it would make his house sturdy. After the foundation was done, he built his house right on top of it. Then one day a huge storm came, and the flood waters rose and beat against the house. But the house didn't budge. Its rock foundation kept it from washing away.

"And this is how you will be if you listen to my words and take them into your hearts."

Then Jesus told them about another builder:

"Another man wanted to build a house, but he didn't think it was worth his time to dig deep and put in a good solid foundation. Instead, he built his house on the sandy soil. But a storm came, the winds began to howl, and the flood waters rose. His house crumbled into pieces and fell to the ground!

"This is how it is for those who hear my words, but do not think it is important to take them into their hearts."

"Love Your Enemies"

Luke 6

*L*isten if you can," said Jesus. He knew His next words would be hard to understand. "I want you to love your enemies. Be good to those who treat you badly. If someone says mean words to you, say kind words to them. If someone slaps you on the cheek, turn and offer them your other cheek. And if someone takes your coat, offer them your shirt as well.

"Give what you can to those who ask. And if someone takes something of yours, don't demand it back. Always treat others the way you would like to be treated. It's easy to love those who love you, but you should also love those who treat you wrong. Because God the Father is loving and kind–and ready to forgive those who do wrong. And God will reward you for doing these things. And He will call you His very own child."

The Good Fruit Tree

Luke 6

A good tree will not grow bad fruit," said Jesus one day. "And you can tell what sort of tree it is by looking at the fruit. Everyone knows you can't pick figs from a thorn bush. And you don't find grapes growing on a briar vine."

Jesus looked into the eyes of His listeners and continued, "You can know if someone is good, kind, and loving when you see them doing good, kind, and loving deeds. These deeds are like a special kind of fruit that grows from their hearts. In the same way you can know when you see someone who acts out of hatred or anger or jealousy that this person has the same kind of evils inside of them."

The Centurion's Faith

Matthew 8

*J*esus went to a town called Capernaum.
There He was met by a worried soldier.
This soldier was called a centurion because he was in charge
of one-hundred other soldiers.

"Lord," said the centurion, "my servant is very sick. He
lies in bed at home and cannot move a muscle."

"I will go and heal him," said Jesus.

"Oh no, Lord," said the centurion, "I don't deserve
to have you come to my house. But I know if you just say
the word, my servant will be healed. Since I'm a soldier I
understand authority. I do what I'm commanded and I also
command others to go and to come, and they obey."

Jesus was astonished at the centurion's words. He turned and spoke to the people around Him.

"The truth is, I have never found anyone in all of Israel with such great faith!"

Jesus turned to the centurion. "Go, right now! Your servant will be healed just as you have believed he would."

And when the centurion arrived home, his servant was completely well!

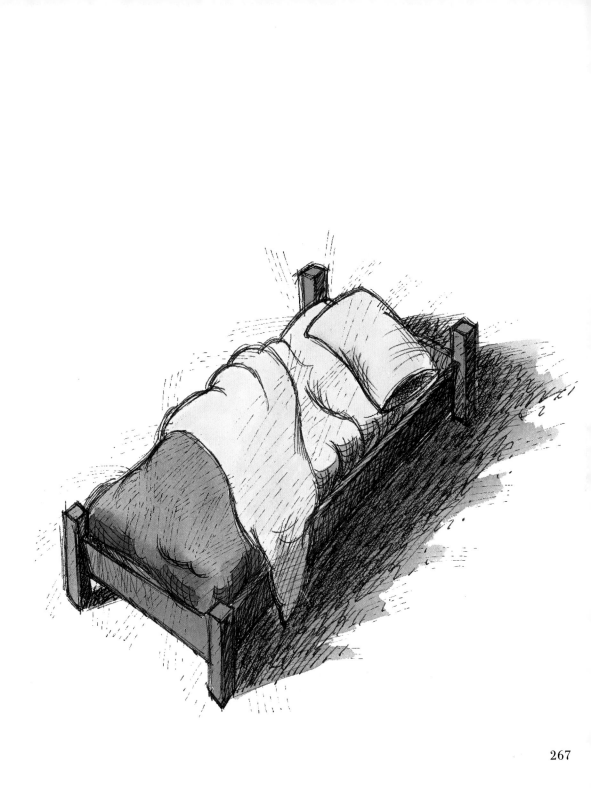

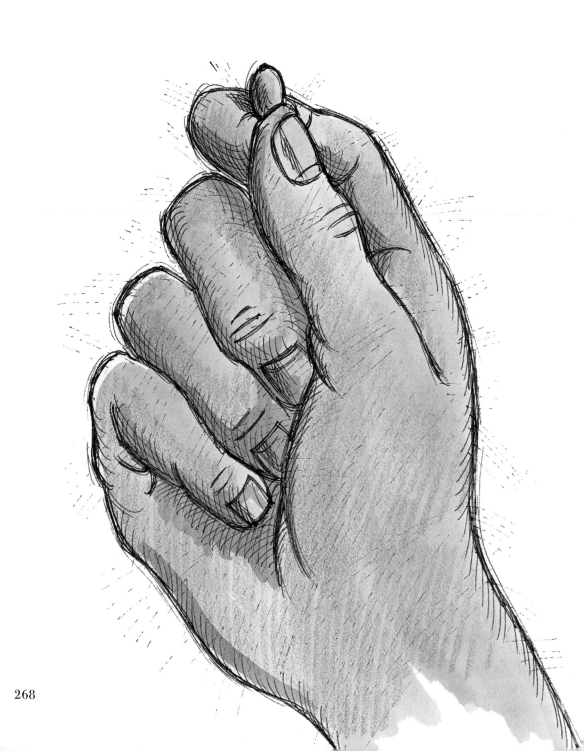

The Mustard Seed

Matthew 13

God's kingdom could be compared to a tiny mustard seed," explained Jesus one day. "It looks so small and unimportant, but inside this little seed is the power to grow into a great, big plant. If you plant this tiny seed along with other vegetable seeds you will be amazed at how quickly this one will grow into a large bushy plant. And before long, it will become the biggest plant in the whole garden. And birds will come and build their nests in it!"

A Priceless Treasure!

Matthew 13

*J*esus told another parable:

"The kingdom of heaven is like a buried treasure," said Jesus. "When a man finds this amazing treasure buried in a field, he quickly hides it again. Then the man joyfully goes out and sells every, single thing he owns. Now he takes his money and buys the field where the treasure is hidden. And the treasure is worth much, much more than everything he gave up to purchase it with!"

A Frightening Storm

L u k e   8

*O*ne day Jesus said to His disciples, "Let's go over to the other side of the lake."

So they all climbed into a boat and began to sail across the water. Jesus settled down in a quiet corner of the boat and soon fell fast asleep. But while He was sleeping a huge and horrible storm began to rage!

High, angry waves smashed with fury into the boat, and the wind howled and screamed! The boat was tossed back and forth with each new wave. It took on more and more sea water until it was almost sinking. The disciples knew they were in danger and feared for their lives. But all the while, Jesus slept peacefully as if nothing whatsoever was wrong.

"Master!" the disciples cried out in despair. "Help us! We are all surely going to drown!"

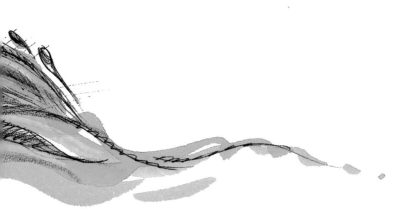

Jesus got up from His nap, and told the raging wind and the fierce waves to be still. Immediately the wind became quiet and the waves grew calm.

"What has happened to your faith?" Jesus asked His disciples. But they were so surprised when the storm stopped that they couldn't even answer Him.

Later they whispered to each other in amazement, "Who can this man possibly be? Even the wind and the waves obey Him!"

The Woman at the Well

John 4

*J*esus sat down by a well to rest while His disciples went to find food. A Samaritan woman came to draw water, and Jesus asked her for a drink. She turned to Him in surprise, for Jews did not usually speak to Samaritans. "You are a Jew," she said. "And I am a Samaritan. Why ask me for water?"

Jesus smiled. "If you knew what God is able to give, or who it is that asks you for a drink, you would have asked Me to give you living water!"

"Sir," she said, "You have no jug, and our well is deep. How can You give me this living water?"

"All who drink this water will thirst again," said Jesus. "Whoever drinks My water won't thirst. My water flows like a fountain, giving eternal life!"

"Please," begged the woman. "Give me Your water! I won't need to come here anymore." First Jesus talked about her life. He knew all about her.

"You're a prophet," she said. "But we Samaritans worship God differently."

"Soon all who worship God will worship Him with their whole heart," said Jesus.

"The Messiah will come and show us," she said.

"I am He," said Jesus.

Feeding the Crowds

John 6

Jesus and His disciples took a boat across the Sea of Galilee, for Jesus wished to get away from the busy towns. But as they sailed, they spotted a huge crowd walking along the shore. When the boat reached the other side, Jesus and the disciples got out and went to the hillside. Jesus saw this crowd coming toward them. He turned to Philip and said, "Where shall we buy food for these people?"

Philip looked up in surprise. "It would take a fortune to feed all these people!" he exclaimed.

"Here's a boy who's willing to share," announced Andrew. "He only has five loaves of bread and two little fish. That couldn't feed many people."

"Tell everyone to sit down," said Jesus with a smile. Soon the huge crowd was seated on the green, grassy slope. Jesus thanked God for the boy's lunch. Then He broke the bread and fish and gave it to the crowd. Everyone ate. Soon they were full!

"Now," said Jesus, "gather all the leftovers, and be sure not to waste any." The disciples filled twelve baskets. And the crowd was amazed!

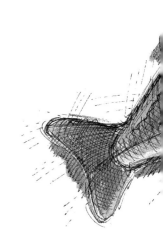

He Walks on Water!

After feeding the huge crowd, Jesus told His disciples to go ahead without Him. He needed time with His Father. So He went to the hills to pray.

As the sun set, the disciples began to sail across the lake. But when it became dark, the wind began to stir the waves, tossing the small boat back and forth. Then in the middle of the night, the disciples noticed something strange. A man walked toward them—right on top of the water!

"It's a ghost!" they cried in terror.

"Don't be afraid!" called Jesus. "It is I."

Peter yelled, "If it's You, Lord, call me out to You!" Jesus called, and Peter climbed out of the boat. He too began to walk on the water. But when his eyes looked away from Jesus and down at the frothing sea, Peter began to sink. "Help me, Lord!" he cried. Jesus grabbed Peter's hand.

"Peter, where's your faith?" asked Jesus as they climbed into the boat.

But Peter and the other disciples could only bow down before Jesus. "You really are the Son of God!" they said.

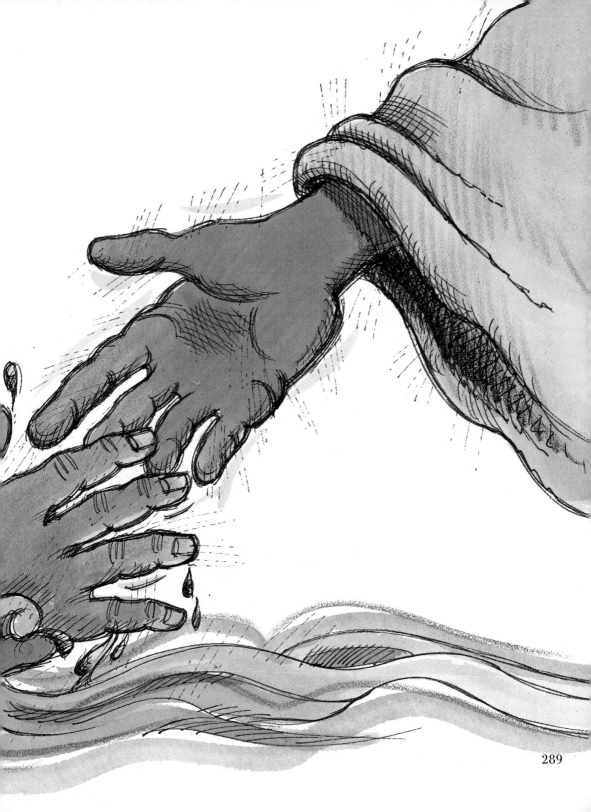

A Good Neighbor

Luke 10

*J*esus told this story to teach what it really means to love your neighbor as yourself:

"One day, a Jewish man was traveling from Jerusalem to Jericho," began Jesus. "But he was attacked by brutal robbers who beat him! They stole his clothes and money. And finally they left him all alone beside the road to die."

"After a while, a Jewish priest came along. He saw the poor, beaten man and heard him groaning. But the priest did not want to be bothered. So he turned his head and went to the other side of the road. He continued on his way. Later on, a Levite came along. And he too saw the bleeding man next to the road, but he did exactly the same as the priest. But then a Samaritan came along," continued Jesus.

The people listened closely—knowing that Jews and Samaritans never got along.

"When this Samaritan saw the injured man, he felt sorry for him. He stopped, bent down, and cleaned and bandaged the man's wounds. Then he lifted the man onto his donkey and took him to a nearby inn. There, he cared for the man. The next day, the Samaritan had to be on his way, but he left money with the innkeeper, saying, 'Please care for this man. When I return, I'll pay you whatever it costs.'

"Which of the three travelers was a good neighbor?" asked Jesus.

The Greatest in God's Kingdom

Matthew 18

*O*ne day, the disciples came to Jesus with a question. "Who will be greatest in God's kingdom?"

Jesus called a child over and said, "This is the truth: unless you become like a little child, you will never enter God's kingdom. Only those who understand how small they are compared to God's greatness will be important in God's kingdom."

A Servant's Heart

Mark 10

*J*esus told His disciples something else about God's way of looking at greatness:

"In this world, you think people are important because they have power or wealth, or because they tell others what to do," said Jesus. "But that's not how it will be for you. To be important in God's kingdom, you must learn to serve. If you want to be at the very top, then you must be like a servant to everyone. Even the Son of God doesn't come to be waited on; He comes to pour out His life for everyone."

Mary and Martha

Luke 10

*J*esus had two friends named Mary and Martha who were sisters. One day, as He traveled, Jesus stopped at Martha's home to visit. Mary was also there. The two sisters were happy to see Jesus. Martha went right to work fixing food and cleaning. She wanted everything perfect for Jesus!

While Martha worked, Mary sat at Jesus' feet, listening to Him. His words were like cool, pure water to Mary. And she gladly drank them in, not wanting to miss a single thing He said.

When Martha noticed how Mary was sitting with Jesus, instead of helping, she became angry. "Lord," exclaimed Martha, "see how Mary just sits while I do all the work. You should tell her to help me!"

"Martha, Martha," said Jesus calmly, "you are bothered by so many little things. Do you know what is really necessary?" Martha looked at Jesus with a puzzled face. "Mary made the right choice," said Jesus. "And it won't be taken from her."

A Rich Fool

L u k e 1 2

ey, Teacher!" called a man in the crowd. "Make my brother split his inheritance with me!"

"Why should I be the judge for you and your brother?" asked Jesus. "But be careful, and watch out for greed. Because having lots of things won't give you a good life." And then He told a story. "There once was a farmer. And one year he harvested an huge crop of grain–his best ever! He was so excited. 'What shall I do now?' he wondered. 'Where shall I store my valuable grain?'

"Then this farmer said, 'I know what I'll do. First I'll tear down my old barns; then I'll build new, bigger, and better ones! Then I'll have lots of room to store my grain and all the terrific things I'll buy with my money!' And so he did this. Then he said to himself, 'Now, I can take it easy– I'll just eat, drink, and be merry!' But God said to him, 'Foolish, foolish man, this very night your life on earth is over. And now what will come of all your worldly riches?'

"And this is what happens," explained Jesus, "to those who only think of getting earthly riches, but are poor when it comes to knowing God."

The Big Party

Luke 14

*J*esus told another story: "A very important man decided to throw a big party," said Jesus. "So he invited many, many friends. And when everything was ready, he sent his servant out to tell his friends it was time to come. But all his friends made excuses—they were too busy to come. When the servant returned and told the man that no one was coming, the man felt very sad.

"The man said to his servant, 'Go out to the streets and back alleys. I want you to look for poor people, blind people, people who are lame or crippled. Invite them all to my party!' The servant did as his master said, but still there was room for more guests at the party. 'Go again,' said the master. 'This time invite everyone who wasn't invited earlier. My house will be full of my new friends!'"

311

A Lost Lamb

Matthew 18

"Think about this," said Jesus: "A man owns a hundred sheep. Every evening, he counts to see that his sheep have come in safely from the hills. But one night, he discovers a little lamb has wandered away and become lost in the dark. Well, do you think that just because this shepherd still has ninety-nine sheep, that he will forget about the one that is missing? No, he goes out into the dark and into the hills, and he searches for his lost lamb.

"The shepherd is overjoyed when he finds his little lamb! He's not thinking about the ninety-nine who are safe and sound. No, he rejoices over this little one that was in danger. And the shepherd carries that lamb upon his shoulders and takes it back to safety. The reason I tell you this story," explained Jesus, "is so you will understand how much your Father in heaven cares about you. He is like that shepherd, and He does not want one single little one to be lost!"

The Blind Man

A crowd followed as Jesus and His disciples approached a town called Jericho. At the edge of town sat a poor blind man named Bartimaeus. When he heard that Jesus was passing by, he began to scream and yell with all his might. "Jesus!" he cried. "Son of David, have mercy on me!" People nearby tried to quiet blind Bartimaeus. But the more they tried, the louder he shouted. "Son of David!" he hollered at the top of his lungs. "Please, have mercy on me!"

Jesus stopped walking and turned to His disciples. "Call that man over to Me," He said.

The disciples went to Bartimaeus. "Cheer up!" they said. "Get on your feet and come with us. Jesus is calling for you." Tossing down his cloak, the blind man leaped up and went with them.

"What do you want me to do?" asked Jesus.

"Teacher," said Bartimaeus, "I wish to see."

"Go," said Jesus. "Because of your faith, you are healed." Instantly, Bartimaeus could see! He followed Jesus, looking at everything as he went!

Zacchaeus the Tax Collector

Zacchaeus was a tax collector who got rich by making others pay lots of taxes. When Zacchaeus heard Jesus was in town, he wanted to see Him. But Zacchaeus was short, and Jesus was always surrounded by a crowd. So Zacchaeus decided to run ahead of the crowd and climb a sycamore tree. From there he could watch for Jesus. He watched as Jesus drew closer. He held his breath when Jesus stopped right beneath his tree. Then Jesus looked straight up at him!

"Zacchaeus," said Jesus with a smile, "come on down. I want to stay at your house today!"

Zacchaeus hopped down. "You are welcome at my house, Jesus," said the little man with a big smile.

But others grumbled, muttering to each other. "Why does Jesus want to go home with a sinner?"

Zacchaeus turned to Jesus and said, "Look, Lord. Here and now, I promise to give half of my money to the poor. If I have cheated anyone in taxes, I will pay them back four times that amount."

"Salvation comes to Zacchaeus's house today!" announced Jesus. "For I have come to look for and to save those who are lost."

A Widow's Gift

Luke 20-21

*J*esus warned His disciples, "Watch out for those who teach the law. They like parading in fancy clothes and being seen in the marketplace. They always want the best. And yet they often treat poor widows unfairly. Men like that will be punished one day."

Jesus looked up and saw a rich man proudly place money into the temple treasury. Then a poor widow quietly dropped two small coins into the box. "The truth is, that poor widow gave more than all the others. The others gave out of much riches, but she gave all the money she has in the world."

The Good Shepherd

J o h n   1 0

One day, Jesus said, "If a man sneaks over the fence to get into a sheep pen, he probably is a thief. If he calls the sheep, they won't come because he's a stranger. His voice frightens them and they run away. But the real shepherd enters through the gate. And when he calls his sheep, he uses their names, and they know his voice.

"I am the good shepherd. I know each of My sheep by name, and My sheep know Me. And I am the gate. Those who come through Me will be saved. They will have everything they need.

"Sometimes a man is hired to watch over the sheep," continued Jesus. "But this man does not own these sheep and he does not really care about them. He just works to get paid. If a wolf comes in the middle of the night, the man runs away! And the wolf attacks the sheep and scatters the flock. The man doesn't even care—because they're not his sheep.

"But I am the good shepherd," said Jesus. "And I lay down My life for My sheep.

"My Father loves Me, and I gladly lay down My life for My sheep. Even though He has told Me to do this, I do it because I want to. No man will take My life from Me. Instead, I give it freely.

"And after I lay down My life, My Father has given Me the power to take it back again."

332

Lazarus, Wake Up!

John 11

*J*esus received a message from Mary and Martha, saying their brother was sick. "This sickness won't be the end," explained Jesus. "It's for God's glory."

After two days, Jesus said he would go to Lazarus. But the disciples were afraid, saying, "But they tried to kill You last time we were in Judea!"

"Yes," said Jesus, "but Lazarus is sleeping and I need to go wake him." The disciples asked if this meant that Lazarus was getting better.

"No," said Jesus, "he is dead. And it's good that I wasn't there. This will help you to believe."

"Let's go even if it means death," said Thomas.

Martha met Jesus at the edge of town. "Lord," she cried, "if You had been here, my brother would be alive. Still, I know God will give You what You ask."

"Lazarus will come back to life," said Jesus.

"I know he will come to life in the resurrection at the last day," said Martha.

"I am the resurrection and the life," said Jesus. "Anyone who believes in Me will live—even if he dies. Do you believe this, Martha?"

"Yes, Lord," she answered. "I believe You are the Christ, the Son of God, the one who will save the world."

Martha went home to tell Mary that Jesus had come. Then Mary hurried to the edge of town, followed by many Jewish friends who had come to comfort the sisters. "Lord," sobbed Mary, "if You had been here, my brother would not have died!"

Jesus looked at Mary and the others who were crying. "Where have you laid Lazarus?" he asked.

"Come, we will show You," they said.

As they walked, Jesus cried too.

"Look," whispered some of the Jewish friends. "He really did love Lazarus."

They stopped before the tomb. "Remove the stone," Jesus commanded, His face wet with tears.

"But Lord," said Martha, "Lazarus has been dead for days. There will be a horrible smell."

"Believe and see God's glory," said Jesus.

The stone was moved, and Jesus prayed. Then, in a loud voice He called, "Lazarus, come out!" The crowd grew silent as they watched and waited.

Out stepped a man wrapped in cloth! Gasps of wonder rippled through the crowd. "Help him remove the grave clothes so he can walk," said Jesus.

Mary's Gift

*M*artha served a special dinner to honor Jesus. Her brother Lazarus was also there. After a while, Mary came in. She opened up a jar of sweet-smelling perfume. It was a very special perfume that was rare and quite valuable. Then to everyone's surprise, Mary poured out this rare perfume— right onto Jesus' feet. And she used her own hair to wipe His feet. This was her way to show how much she loved Jesus. And this wonderful fragrance filled the entire house!

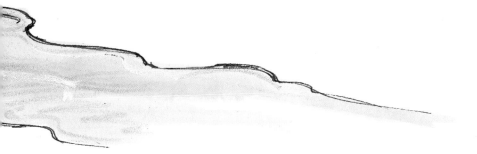

"Mary, what have you done?" cried Judas Iscariot. "You've wasted all that costly perfume! It should have been sold and the money given to the poor." But Judas was thinking only of himself. He was the money-keeper for Jesus and the disciples–and when no one was looking, he often stole from them.

"Let her be," said Jesus gently. "Mary has done what is right and good. This perfume is to be my burial ointment. You see, I will not be with you much longer. But you will always be able to give to the poor."

Entering Jerusalem
Mark 11

*J*esus came to a small village near Jerusalem. He told two of His disciples, "Go into that town, and near the entrance you will find a colt that has never been ridden. Untie the colt and bring it back. If anyone asks you what you are doing, tell them that the Lord needs the colt and that He will return it later."

The two did as Jesus said, and soon returned with the colt. Then the disciples laid their garments on the colt like a saddle, and Jesus sat on the colt and began to ride.

As Jesus entered Jerusalem, people lay their coats and garments across the road before Him. Others spread palm branches they had cut from the nearby trees. A joyful parade followed Jesus as He rode the young colt through Jerusalem. The celebration continued as the crowd waved and shouted praises.

"Hosanna! Hosanna!" they cried. "Blessed is He who comes in the name of the Lord! Hosanna in the highest!"

The Servant of All

John 13

*R*ight before Passover, Jesus shared a special meal with His disciples. It was almost time to return to the Father, and Jesus wanted to show His disciples how much He loved them. So He wrapped a towel around His waist and poured water into a bowl, just as a servant would do. Then He knelt before Simon Peter.

"No!" said Peter. "You can't wash my feet."

"If I don't wash you, you are not part of Me," explained Jesus.

"Oh," said Peter, "then wash all of me!"

"Only your feet need be washed," said Jesus as He continued washing. "You see, a person who has already bathed is clean, but his feet get dirty when he walks along the road." After Jesus washed all the disciples' feet, He sat back down.

"Do you know why I did this?" He asked. "You call me Lord, and that is right. But today I gave you something to remember. See how I served you. I want you to serve each other in the same way. And if you do these things, you will be blessed."

The Betrayer

Matthew 26

*J*udas Iscariot heard that the high priests wanted to get rid of Jesus. And Judas knew they had lots of money. So he went to the priests and asked, "What will you give me if I turn Jesus over to you?"

The high priests gave Judas thirty silver coins. And from then on, Judas looked for a chance to betray Jesus.

Jesus Knows

J o h n   1 3

*J*esus told His disciples that one of them would betray Him. "It is meant to happen," He explained. "Scripture says that the one who eats bread with Me will also betray Me. I'm telling you now, so that when it happens you will understand."

A disciple who dearly loved Jesus leaned over and asked, "Who is the betrayer, Lord?"

"I will dip this bread and give it to the one," said Jesus. Then He dipped the bread and handed it to Judas Iscariot.

When Judas took the bread from Jesus, Satan entered into him.

"Go quickly," said Jesus to Judas. "Do what you must do."

Judas Iscariot left Jesus and the other disciples. And Judas went out by himself—out into the darkness of the night.

The Lord's Supper

Matthew 26, John 13

*J*esus continued to eat supper with the remaining eleven disciples. As they ate, Jesus held up a piece of bread. First He gave thanks for it, then He broke it into pieces and shared it with His disciples.

"Take and eat this," He said. "This is My body."

Then Jesus took a cup of wine and gave thanks for it. He shared it with His disciples, saying, "Drink from this cup. This is My blood which will be poured out so that many can receive forgiveness for their sins.

"I will not drink any fruit of the vine until I drink it together with you, when we meet again in My Father's house."

362

"Not Me, Lord"

*L*ove each other the way I have loved you," said Jesus. "When people see how much you love each other, they will know you are My disciples."

"But where are You going?" asked Simon Peter.

"You cannot go with Me now," said Jesus.

"Why can't I follow You?" asked Peter. "I would lay down my life for You!"

"Peter," said Jesus, "before the rooster crows tomorrow morning, you will deny Me three times."

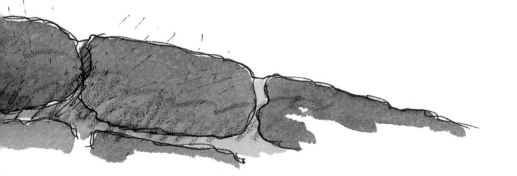

My Father's House

John 14

Don't be worried," said Jesus. "Just trust God. He has a huge house with many, many rooms. And I am going to get your place ready. Then I'll come back for you!"

"How will we get there?" asked Thomas.

"I am the way," said Jesus. "I am the truth and the life. No one comes to the Father except through Me. If you see Me, you see the Father. When I go to the Father, you can ask anything in My name, and I will do it to bring glory to the Father."

Like a Vine

J o h n 1 5

I am like a vine," said Jesus, "and you are like My branches. I want you to cling to Me in the same way that a branch clings to a vine. My Father is like the gardener who will prune and care for the vine. When the branches are healthy they bear good fruit. They are part of the vine. That's how I want you to be– a part of me.

"I love you the same way My Father loves me. Stay in My love. Let My love stay in you."

In the Garden

Matthew 26

*T*hat night, Jesus took His disciples to a quiet garden called Gethsemane. "Stay here and pray while I go over there," said Jesus to some of the disciples. Then He turned to Peter, James, and John, and said, "My heart is breaking with sadness. Stay here to watch and pray."

Jesus went on ahead of them. Falling with His face to the ground, He cried out to the Father. "If it is possible, please remove this task from Me. But don't do My will, Father; only let Your will be done."

When Jesus returned to His disciples, He found that they had all fallen asleep. And so, in His darkest hour, Jesus prayed alone. He cried out to His Father again and again.

Finally, He finished praying. He went back and woke up His disciples. "The time has come for the Son of Man to be betrayed!" He said. "Look, here comes My betrayer now!"

Arrested!

Luke 22, Mark 14

*M*en armed with swords and clubs marched to where Jesus and the disciples stood. The angry crowd was led by Judas Iscariot, who had already set up a signal–he would kiss the man they were to arrest. When Judas kissed Jesus, Jesus asked, "Judas, do you betray the Son of Man with a kiss?"

Immediately the guards seized Jesus! Then Simon Peter grabbed a sword and cut off the ear of the high priest's servant.

"That is enough," said Jesus. Then He touched the servant and healed his ear. Jesus turned to the priests and temple guards. "Am I leading a rebellion that you come with weapons and force? You did nothing all those times I spoke in the temple. But this is your time–when darkness rules!"

Then they took Jesus to the home of the high priest to be questioned. The frightened disciples all ran away.

Peter Denies Jesus

Matthew 26, Luke 22

*P*eter was warming himself by a fire in the high priest's courtyard when a servant girl asked, "Weren't you with Jesus?"

"I don't know Him," said Peter. Later, someone else asked the same thing, and once again Peter denied knowing Jesus.

An hour later, another man spoke to Peter. "Surely you're one of Jesus' followers. You even talk like them."

"I don't know what you're talking about!" cried Peter. Just then a rooster crowed, and Peter remembered Jesus' words. Moments later, as Jesus was being led by the guards, He turned and looked at Peter. Peter went away and cried bitterly.

Jesus is Questioned

Luke 22

The guards beat Jesus with whips and sticks. They covered His eyes with a blindfold and struck Him. "If You're a prophet," they yelled, "tell us who is hitting You now!" Then they spat on Him.

After that, Jesus was questioned. "Tell us if You are the Christ," demanded the high priest.

"If I say so," said Jesus, "you will not believe Me. And if I ask, you will not answer. But from now on, the Son of Man will sit at the right hand of God."

"So," they said, "are You the Son of God?"

"You are right," said Jesus. "I am."

"There!" they said. "We've heard enough!"

Pilate & Herod

Luke 23

*T*hen the priests and elders bound Jesus with ropes and had Him dragged before the Roman governor, Pilate.

"So are You the King of the Jews?" Pilate asked.

"Yes," said Jesus. "It is as you say."

Pilate asked a few more questions, then turned to the people and said, "I see no reason to punish this Man." But the priests and elders didn't like that answer. And so Pilate sent Jesus to stand before Herod.

Herod asked Jesus lots of questions, hoping that Jesus would perform a miracle. But Jesus remained silent. So Herod and his soldiers cruelly mocked Jesus, then sent Him back to Pilate.

"I still see no reason to kill this Man," said Pilate to the Jewish leaders. But they would not listen. They demanded that Jesus be killed.

"But why?" cried Pilate. "For what crime?"

"Crucify Him!" cried the angry crowd. "Crucify Him!"

The Cross

Luke 23

*S*oldiers placed a crown of thorns on Jesus' head, then mocked Him, saying, "Hail, King of the Jews!" Then they led Jesus to a place of death called The Skull. They nailed His hands and feet to a rough wooden cross. Two criminals also hung on crosses, one on each side of Jesus.

From the cross, Jesus looked down on the people–the very ones who were killing Him–and said, "Forgive them, Father, for they don't know what they are doing."

Some of the people made fun of Jesus, calling out, "You saved others; now see if You can save yourself!" Even the man on the cross next to Jesus joined in the mocking.

But the man on the other cross stopped him. "Man, you are about to die! Don't you fear God at all? We did horrible things. We deserve to die. But Jesus is innocent." He turned to Jesus. "Please, Jesus, remember me when You come into Your kingdom."

"This day, you will join Me in paradise," Jesus answered.

387

The Darkest Hour

Luke 23

*A*nd then, although it was still the middle of the day, darkness swallowed the sunlight. And the air became still.

"Father!" cried Jesus. "Into Your hands I commit My spirit!" Then Jesus breathed His last breath. And in that black and lonely moment, Jesus died.

The earth grew deathly silent, and the sky remained hopelessly dark. And down in Jerusalem, the great curtain in the temple was ripped from top to bottom!

"Surely this was righteous man," said a centurion. Those who loved Jesus stood off in the distance crying.

He Lives!

Matthew 27-28, John 20

*J*oseph was a rich man who had followed Jesus. Joseph asked Pilate if he could care for Jesus' body, and Pilate agreed. Joseph made sure that Jesus' body was wrapped in a clean white cloth and laid in a special tomb carved from solid rock. Then a large stone was placed in front of the opening to the tomb.

The Pharisees asked Pilate to place guards at the tomb to make sure that no one could steal Jesus' body.

After the Sabbath, Mary Magdalene went to the tomb early in the morning while it was still dark. When she reached the tomb, she found that the stone was rolled away! She turned and ran back down the road until she came to Peter and John.

"They have taken our Lord out of the tomb!" she cried. "I don't know where they have put Him!"

The disciples ran on to the tomb, and found the strips of white cloth that had been on Jesus. But Jesus was gone! They didn't know what to think. The disciples returned to their homes.

Mary remained at the tomb, crying. But when she looked up, she saw two angels dressed in white.

"Why are you crying, Mary?" asked the angels.

"They took my Lord. I don't know where they have put Him." Then Mary saw a man. She thought He was the gardener. "Sir," she asked, "if You have taken Him away, please tell me–"

"Mary," He said. And instantly, Mary realized it was Jesus standing right in front of her!

"Teacher!" she cried.

"Do not touch Me," said Jesus, "for I haven't been to the Father yet. But go and tell the others that I am returning to My Father, who is also your Father." So Mary ran and told the others that Jesus was alive! Jesus had risen from the dead!

Thomas Has Doubts

J o h n 2 0

*D*uring the next few days, many of the disciples saw Jesus. But Thomas did not see Him. And so Thomas had a hard time believing that Jesus had really risen from the dead. Thomas told the others, "Unless I see the holes in His hands where the nails went through, I won't believe that Jesus is alive."

A week later, Jesus appeared to the disciples again. And this time Thomas was there. "Touch the holes in My hands," said Jesus as He showed Thomas the nail holes. "Now stop doubting and believe."

"You are my Lord and God," said Thomas.

A Big Catch of Fish

John 21

One morning, some of the disciples decided to go back to fishing. But they fished all night without catching a thing.

Someone called from the shore, "Catching any fish?"

"None," they called back.

"Try tossing your net on the right side of the boat," called the stranger. And when they did, the net became so full of fish that they could hardly drag it back into the boat.

"It's Jesus!" shouted John. Then Peter dived into the sea and swam to shore. The others followed in the boat. When they all gathered on the shore, Jesus shared breakfast with them.

Peter's Second Chance

J o h n   2 1

*T*hen Jesus turned to Peter and said, "Peter, do you love Me?"

"Yes," said Peter. "You know I love You."

"Then feed My lambs," said Jesus. Again, He asked Peter, "Do you really love Me?"

"Yes, Lord," said Peter. "You know that I love You."

"Then take care of My sheep," said Jesus. And for the third time, Jesus asked him, "Peter, do you love Me?"

Peter felt bad because Jesus had asked him this question three times. (And Peter knew he had denied Jesus three times.) Peter cried out, "Lord, You know everything; surely You must know that I love You."

"Then feed My sheep," said Jesus.

A Job To Do

Matthew 28, Mark 16

*J*esus told His disciples to meet Him on a mountain, and there He gave them a special job to do.

"Go into all the world," said Jesus, "and tell everyone the good news. Teach others how to be My disciples. Show them how to do the things that I have taught you. And baptize them in the name of the Father and of the Son and of the Holy Spirit.

"And remember this: I will always be with you – even to the very end of time."

Jesus Sends a Helper

A c t s   2

*M*any days later, the disciples gathered in one place. Suddenly a sound like a loud, roaring wind whipped through the room and shook the entire house! The disciples stared in wonder as a small flame of fire came to rest on each one of them. And in that same moment, they were all filled with the Holy Spirit—the one that Jesus had promised. The power they received from the Holy Spirit made them able to speak in languages they had never known before.

The disciples poured out into the streets, speaking their new languages. Jerusalem was filled with visitors from all over the world. And when they heard the disciples talking about God in their own languages, they were completely amazed.

Peter spoke to the huge crowd, telling how the ancient Jewish prophets had known that God would send Jesus to forgive their sins. Then Peter told about how Jesus had died and come back to life, and how they too could be saved.

And 3,000 people listened to this message and were baptized that very day!

Rise Up and Walk!

Acts 3

*O*ne day, Peter and John went to the temple to pray. But when they reached the gates, they saw a man who couldn't walk because his legs were paralyzed. Each day this man's friends would set him by the temple gates to beg for money.

"Please," begged the man. "Can you help the poor?"

Peter and John both stopped.

"Look at us," said Peter. And the man looked up, holding his hand out for money.

Peter looked at the man and said, "I do not have any silver or gold. But I do have this." Then Peter bent down and took the man's hand and said, "In the name of Jesus Christ, I say to you, rise up and walk!"

The man leaped to his feet in joy! And he went with them to the temple, walking and jumping and praising God all the way. Everyone who had known this man stared in wonder.

Philip Makes a New Friend

Acts 8

*O*ne day, an angel told Philip to travel on a road that went into the desert. On his way, Philip met an important Ethiopian man who had been to Jerusalem to worship God. This man was reading the words of the old prophets, but didn't know what they meant.

"How can I understand this unless someone explains it to me?" asked the Ethiopian. Philip told the man all about Jesus, and how He had come just like the prophets had said He would.

The Ethiopian was moved by Philip's words about Jesus. It was clear that God had sent Philip to tell the Ethiopian this good news.

"Please," said the Ethiopian, pointing to a water hole. "Let's stop right here, and you can baptize me." So Philip baptized his new friend. After that, the Ethiopian went on his way rejoicing. And God took Philip on to tell many, many others about Jesus.

Saul Sees the Light

A c t s 9

A man named Saul hated the followers of Jesus. He wanted to see them all locked up in prison. One day, as Saul traveled to Damascus, a bright light from heaven flashed down upon him and he fell to the ground.

"Saul! Saul!" said a voice. "Why do you hate Me so?"

"Who are You?" asked Saul.

"I am Jesus," replied the voice. "Now get up and go to the city. You'll be told what you must do." But when Saul got up, he could not see. He was completely blind! He was led to Damascus. And for three days Saul did not eat or drink. He only prayed.

Finally, God sent Ananias to visit Saul. Ananias was worried, because he knew that Saul hated Jesus' followers. But he went, just as God told him. He put his hands on Saul and prayed. Instantly, Saul was able to see again. He was baptized, and then spent time learning about Jesus from the disciples. Soon Saul was telling everyone about Jesus—the same Man he used to hate. Saul was like a brand-new man, and he began to go by a new name. He became known as Paul.

Paul's Shipwreck Adventure

Acts 27 - 28

*P*aul became a mighty preacher for Jesus, telling everyone far and wide about Jesus. But when he went to Jerusalem to preach, the Jews made trouble for him. He was beaten and arrested again and again. But that didn't stop Paul! And each time he stood before the officials, he told how Jesus had changed his life. So more and more people heard the good news.

Finally, Paul was put on a ship with other prisoners. When a horrible storm came up, God showed Paul that the ship would be wrecked, but everyone who stayed on board would be spared and make it safely to an island. Paul told the others about this.

It happened just as Paul said. The ship was wrecked, but they all made it safely to the island of Malta. On the island, Paul gathered some wood for a fire, but a deadly snake jumped out and bit him! The islanders said, "That prisoner must be very bad. Now he will get what he deserves." But when Paul didn't even get sick, they said, "This man must be a god." Then Paul was invited to stay in the home of an important man. The man's father was very ill, but when Paul prayed, the man was healed.

God used Paul's shipwreck to bring the good news to the island of Malta. And when Paul was put back in prison, God helped him write letters to encourage others.

The Holy City

Revelation 21

*A*nother one of Jesus' disciples spent some time on an island, too. And while he was there, God showed him what it will be like when Jesus takes His believers home to heaven.

There will be a new heaven and a new earth. All sadness and crying and sickness and death will be gone. The new city of God will be enormous—and more beautiful than anything you've ever seen. A spectacular wall will surround the city like a glittering rainbow made of millions of colorful jewels. And there will be twelve giant gates in the wall, each made of solid pearl. The streets will be polished gold that glistens like glass. And the buildings will be of shimmering gold and glass.

Jesus Is Coming Back!

Revelation 22

And there will be no need for a temple, for the Father and Son will be there. And there will be no need for sun or moon, for God's glory will be brighter than the summer sun!

A crystal-clear river of life will flow from the throne of God and through the city. The tree of life will grow there, bringing forth new fruit each month. And the leaves of this tree will heal all the nations.

Jesus said, "Behold, I am coming soon! I am the First and the Last, the Beginning and the End. Yes, I am coming soon."

Amen. Come, Lord Jesus.

Topical Index

Angels

Jacob's Dream	74
Gideon	128
Samson	132
Daniel and the Lions	194
An Angel's Visit	204
Joseph's Dream	208
The Shepherds' Surprise!	214
Tempted in the Wilderness	230

Anger

Cain and Abel	44
Jacob Tricks Esau	72

Animals

Creatures of the Deep	22
Wings to Fly	26
Here Come the Animals!	28
Jonah and the Big Fish	198
Born in a Stable	212

Babies

The Serpent's Lie	40
Abraham Obeys God	56
Jacob and Esau	68
Joseph	78
Baby Moses	90
Hannah's Prayer	142
An Angel's Visit	204
Mary Visits Elizabeth	206
Joseph's Dream	208
Born in a Stable	212
The Shepherds' Surprise!	214
Wise Men from the East	216

Baptism

Jesus is Baptized	226
Jesus Sends a Helper	404
Philip Makes a New Friend	412

Battles

Jericho	122
Gideon	128
Samson	132
David and Goliath	156
Tempted in the Wilderness	230

Bethlehem

Ruth and Naomi	136
To Bethlehem	210
The Shepherds' Surprise!	214
Wise Men from the East	216

Betrayal

The Serpent's Lie	40
Cain and Abel	44
Jacob Tricks Esau	72
Joseph	78
Samson	132
Queen Esther	182
Daniel and the Lions	194
Jesus Knows	299
The Betrayer	352
Arrested!	372
Jesus is Questioned	378

Birds

Wings to Fly	26
Elijah	168
Things to Remember	248

Blessings

Jacob and Esau	68
Jacob Tricks Esau	72
Jacob's Dream	74
Food from Heaven	110
Water in the Desert	112
Hannah's Prayer	142
An Angel's Visit	204

Boats

Noah Builds a Boat	46
Baby Moses	90
Jonah and the Big Fish	198
"Come Follow Me"	234
A Frightening Storm	272
He Walks on Water!	286
A Big Catch of Fish	398
Paul's Shipwreck Adventure	420

Bravery

Moses Runs Away	94
Moses Leads His People	104
Twelve Explorers	116
Jericho	122
Gideon	128
Samson	132
David and Goliath	156
David the King	160
Queen Esther	182
The Fiery Furnace	190
Daniel and the Lions	194
The Cross	384

Brothers

Cain and Abel	44
Noah Builds a Boat	46
Jacob and Esau	68
Jacob Tricks Esau	72
Joseph	78
A Plea for Help	86
"Come Follow Me"	234
Lazarus, Wake Up!	332

Building

Noah Builds a Boat	46
The Tower of Babel	54
David the King	160
Solomon	164
Two Builders	256

Camels

Isaac and Rebekah	64

Children

Joseph	78
Hannah's Prayer	142
Samuel	146
David	154
Jesus Visits His Father's House	222
The Greatest in God's Kingdom	296

Creation

Let There Be Light	10
The Sky and Sea	14
And Things Began to Grow	18
Creatures of the Deep	22
Wings to Fly	26

Here Come the Animals!   28
God Makes Man   34
God Makes Woman   38

Cross
The Cross   384

Daughters
Jacob and Rachel   76

Death
The Serpent's Lie   40
Plagues, Plagues, and More Plagues   98
The Fiery Furnace   190
Lazarus, Wake Up!   332
"Not Me, Lord"   362
The Cross   384
The Darkest Hour   388

Deception
The Serpent's Lie   40
Jacob Tricks Esau   72
Jacob and Rachel   76
Samson   132
Tempted in the Wilderness   230

Denial
Peter Denies Jesus   376

Desert
Moses Runs Away   94
Moses Leads His People   104
Food from Heaven   110
Water in the Desert   112

Disciples
"Come Follow Me"   234
Jesus' First Miracle   240
Mountaintop Teaching   244
Feeding the Crowds   282
He Walks on Water!   286
Entering Jerusalem   344
The Servant of All   348
The Lord's Supper   358
"Not Me, Lord."   362
Like a Vine   366
In the Garden   368
A Big Catch of Fish   398
Peter's Second Chance   400
Jesus Sends a Helper   404
Rise Up and Walk!   408
Philip Makes a New Friend   412

Donkeys
King Saul   150
Entering Jerusalem   344

Doubt
Moses Leads His People   104
Twelve Explorers   116
Elisha Helps Naaman   178
Jonah and the Big Fish   198
Things to Remember   248
He Walks on Water!   286
Thomas Has Doubts   396

Dreams

Jacob's Dream 74

Joseph 78

Joseph in Egypt 82

Joseph's Dream 208

Earth

Let There Be Light 10

Noah Builds a Boat 46

Egypt

Joseph in Egypt 82

A Plea for Help 86

Baby Moses 90

Moses Leads His People 104

Wise Men from the East 216

Enemies

Baby Moses 90

Jericho 122

Gideon 128

David the King 160

Queen Esther 182

The Fiery Furnace 190

Daniel and the Lions 194

Tempted in the Wilderness 230

"Love Your Enemies" 260

Jesus is Questioned 378

Paul's Shipwreck Adventure 420

Faith

Moses Runs Away 94

Moses Leads His People 104

Jericho 122

Gideon 128

A Fiery Test 174

Elisha Helps Naaman 178

The Fiery Furnace 190

Daniel and the Lions 194

Jesus' First Miracle 240

The Centurion's Faith 264

The Mustard Seed 268

A Frightening Storm 272

He Walks on Water! 286

Lazarus, Wake Up! 332

Thomas Has Doubts 396

Rise Up and Walk! 408

Paul's Shipwreck Adventure 420

Families

A Plea for Help 86

Baby Moses 90

Ruth and Naomi 136

Solomon 164

Mary Visits Elizabeth 206

Joseph's Dream 208

To Bethlehem 210

Born in a Stable 212

Jesus Visits His Father's House 222

Feeding the Crowds 282

Mary and Martha 300

Lazarus, Wake Up! 332

Fathers

The Great Flood 50

Abraham Obeys God 56

Jacob's Dream 74

Joseph 78

A Plea for Help	86
David the King	160
Joseph's Dream	208
To Bethlehem	210
Born in a Stable	212
Jesus Visits His Father's House	222
My Father's House	364

Fear

Moses Leads His People	104
Jonah and the Big Fish	198
A Frightening Storm	272
He Walks on Water!	286
Paul's Shipwreck Adventure	420

Fire

Moses Runs Away	94
A Fiery Test	174
The Fiery Furnace	190

Fish

Creatures of the Deep	22
Jonah and the Big Fish	198
Feeding the Crowds	282
A Big Catch of Fish	398

Fishermen

"Come Follow Me"	234
A Big Catch of Fish	398

Floods

Noah Builds a Boat	46
The Great Flood	50
Two Builders	256

Food

And Things Began to Grow	18
Joseph in Egypt	82
A Plea for Help	86
Food from Heaven	110
Ruth and Naomi	136
Elijah	168
The Widow at Zarephath	170
Queen Esther	182
Tempted in the Wilderness	230
Jesus' First Miracle	240
Things to Remember	248
Feeding the Crowds	282
The Lord's Supper	358
A Big Catch of Fish	398

Foolishness

Two Builders	256
A Rich Fool	304

Forgiveness

A Plea for Help	86
Things to Remember	248
"Love Your Enemies"	260
The Woman at the Well	278
Zacchaeus the Tax Collector	320
The Cross	384
Thomas Has Doubts	396

Friends

God Makes Woman	38
Ruth and Naomi	136
Elijah and Elisha	176
Queen Esther	182
The Fiery Furnace	190

Mary Visits Elizabeth	206		Wise Men from the East	216
"Come Follow Me"	234		Mountaintop Teaching	244
Lazarus, Wake Up!	332		A Widow's Gift	324
Mary's Gift	340		Mary's Gift	340
The Lord's Supper	358		Jesus Sends a Helper	404
My Father's House	364			
Peter's Second Chance	400			
Philip Makes a New Friend	412		**Healing**	
			Elisha Helps Naaman	178
Fruit			The Centurion's Faith	264
And Things Began to Grow	18		A Good Neighbor	290
God Makes Man	34		The Blind Man	316
God Makes Woman	38		Lazarus, Wake Up!	332
The Serpent's Lie	40		Rise Up and Walk!	408
The Good Fruit Tree	262		Saul Sees the Light	416
Like a Vine	366			
			Heaven	
Gardens			Let There Be Light	10
And Things Began to Grow	18		The Tower of Babel	54
God Makes Man	34		Jacob's Dream	74
God Makes Woman	38		Food from Heaven	110
Things to Remember	248		Elijah and Elisha	176
The Mustard Seed	268		Jesus is Baptized	226
Like a Vine	366		The Mustard Seed	268
In the Garden	368		A Priceless Treasure	270
			A Rich Fool	304
Giants			The Big Party	308
David and Goliath	156		My Father's House	364
			A Job to Do	402
Gifts			The Holy City	424
Cain and Abel	44		Jesus Is Coming Back	426
Isaac and Rebekah	64			
Moses Leads His People	104		**Helping**	
Food from Heaven	110		Jericho	122
			Ruth and Naomi	136

David and Goliath 156

The Widow at Zarephath 170

Elisha Helps Naaman 178

Queen Esther 182

Jesus' First Miracle 240

Mountaintop Teaching 244

Things to Remember 248

A Good Neighbor 290

Mary and Martha 300

A Job To Do 402

Jesus Sends a Helper 404

Philip Makes a New Friend 412

Hiding

Baby Moses 90

Moses Runs Away 94

Jericho 122

Elijah 168

Jonah and the Big Fish 198

Holy Spirit

Elijah and Elisha 176

An Angel's Visit 204

Jesus is Baptized 226

Jesus Sends a Helper 404

Honesty

Ten Commandments 114

Samuel 146

Elisha Helps Naaman 178

Queen Esther 182

Houses

Two Builders 256

Hunger

Joseph in Egypt 82

Food from Heaven 110

Jealousy

Cain and Abel 44

Joseph 78

David the King 160

Wise Men from the East 216

Mary and Martha 300

Jerusalem

David the King 160

Wise Men from the East 216

Entering Jerusalem 344

Jesus Sends a Helper 404

Journeys

Abraham Obeys God 56

Joseph in Egypt 82

Moses Runs Away 94

Moses Leads His People 104

Twelve Explorers 116

Ruth and Naomi 136

Hannah's Prayer 142

King Saul 150

Elisha Helps Naaman 178

Jonah and the Big Fish 198

Mary Visits Elizabeth 206

To Bethlehem 210

Wise Men from the East 216

Jesus Visits His Father's House 222
A Good Neighbor 290
Philip Makes a New Friend 412
Paul's Shipwreck Adventure 420

Kings

Samuel 146
King Saul 150
David 154
David and Goliath 156
David the King 160
Solomon 164
Elijah 168
Queen Esther 182
The Fiery Furnace 190
Daniel and the Lions 194
Wise Men from the East 216

Languages

The Tower of Babel 54
Jesus Sends a Helper 404

Light

Let There Be Light 10
Saul Sees the Light 416

Lions

David and Goliath 156
Daniel and the Lions 194

Listening

Mary and Martha 300
The Good Shepherd 326
Jesus Sent a Helper 404

Love

Isaac and Rebekah 64
Jacob and Rachel 76
Jesus is Baptized 226
"Love Your Enemies" 260
A Good Neighbor 290
The Greatest in God's Kingdom 296
The Good Shepherd 326
Mary's Gift 340
The Lord's Supper 358
Like a Vine 366
Peter's Second Chance 400

Loyalty

A Plea for Help 86
Jericho 122
Ruth and Naomi 136
Samuel 146
David and Goliath 156
Elijah 168
The Fiery Furnace 190
Daniel and the Lions 194
A Lost Lamb 312
The Good Shepherd 326
Mary's Gift 340
In the Garden 368
Peter's Second Chance 400

Man

God Makes Man 34

Manna

Food from Heaven 110

Marriage

God Makes Man	34
God Makes Woman	38
Isaac and Rebekah	64
Jacob and Rachel	76
Ruth and Naomi	136
Queen Esther	182
Joseph's Dream	208
Jesus' First Miracle	240

Meals

Jacob and Esau	68
Jacob Tricks Esau	72
Food from Heaven	110
Elijah	168
The Widow at Zarephath	170
Queen Esther	182
Feeding the Crowds	282
Mary and Martha	300
Zacchaeus the Tax Collector	320
The Servant of All	348
The Lord's Supper	358
A Big Catch of Fish	398

Miracles

Moses Runs Away	94
Plagues, Plagues, and More Plagues	98
Moses Leads His People	104
Food from Heaven	110
Water in the Desert	112
Ten Commandments	114
Jericho	122
Gideon	128
Samson	132

Hannah's Prayer	142
David and Goliath	156
Elijah	168
The Widow at Zarephath	170
A Fiery Test	174
Elisha Helps Naaman	178
The Fiery Furnace	190
Daniel and the Lions	194
An Angel's Visit	204
Mary Visits Elizabeth	206
Joseph's Dream	208
Born in a Stable	212
Jesus' First Miracle	240
A Frightening Storm	272
He Walks on Water!	286
A Big Catch of Fish	398
Jesus Sends a Helper	404
Rise Up and Walk!	408
Saul Sees the Light	416
Paul's Shipwreck Adventure	420

Mothers

The Serpent's Lie	40
Jacob and Esau	68
Jacob Tricks Esau	72
Baby Moses	90
Samson	132
Ruth and Naomi	136
Hannah's Prayer	142
The Widow at Zarephath	170
An Angel's Visit	204
Born in a Stable	212
Jesus Visits His Father's House	222
Jesus' First Miracle	240

Mountains

The Great Flood   50

Abraham and Isaac   60

Ten Commandments   114

Tempted in the Wilderness   230

Mountaintop Teaching   244

Neighbors

A Good Neighbor   290

Obeying

Noah Builds a Boat   46

Abraham Obeys God   56

Abraham and Isaac   60

Moses Runs Away   94

Moses Leads His People   104

Jericho   122

Gideon   128

Hannah's Prayer   142

Samuel   146

Solomon   164

Elisha Helps Naaman   178

The Fiery Furnace   190

Daniel and the Lions   194

Jonah and the Big Fish   198

An Angel's Visit   204

Tempted in the Wilderness   230

In the Garden   368

Peter's Second Chance   400

Pharaoh

Joseph in Egypt   82

Baby Moses   90

Moses Runs Away   94

Plagues, Plagues, and More Plagues   98

Moses Leads His People   104

Plagues

Plagues, Plagues, and More Plagues   98

Prayer

Jacob's Dream   74

Solomon   164

Daniel and the Lions   194

"The Lord's Prayer"   244

Things to Remember   248

In the Garden   368

Promised Land

Moses Leads His People   104

Food from Heaven   110

Water in the Desert   112

Twelve Explorers   116

Promises

The Great Flood   50

Jacob's Dream   74

Moses Leads His People   104

Jericho   122

Hannah's Prayer   142

Solomon   164

Elijah and Elisha   176

Peter's Second Chance   400

Jesus Sends a Helper   404

Prophets

Joseph   78

Samuel   146

King Saul 150

Elijah 168

The Widow at Zarephath 170

A Fiery Test 174

Elijah and Elisha 176

Elisha Helps Naaman 178

Jesus is Baptized 226

The Holy City 424

Jesus Is Coming Back! 426

Queens

Queen Esther 182

Rain

The Great Flood 50

Joseph in Egypt 82

Elijah 168

Two Builders 256

Rainbow

The Great Flood 50

Resurrection

He Lives! 390

Thomas Has Doubts 396

Riches

Solomon 164

A Rich Fool 304

A Widow's Gift 324

The Betrayer 352

Rivers

The Sky and Sea 14

Creatures of the Deep 22

Baby Moses 90

Jesus is Baptized 226

Rules

Ten Commandments 114

Sacrifice

Abraham and Isaac 60

The Cross 384

Seas

The Sky and Sea 14

Creatures of the Deep 22

Moses Leads His People 104

A Frightening Storm 272

He Walks on Water! 286

Paul's Shipwreck Adventure 420

Seeds

The Story of the Seeds 252

The Mustard Seed 268

Serpent

The Serpent's Lie 40

Servants

Elisha Helps Naaman 178

An Angel's Visit 204

The Greatest in God's Kingdom 296

A Servant's Heart 299

The Servant of All 348

Sharing

Ruth and Naomi	136
A Good Neighbor	290
Philip Makes a New Friend	412

Sheep (lambs)

Cain and Abel	44
A Lost Lamb	312
The Good Shepherd	326

Shepherds

Moses Runs Away	94
David	154
David the King	160
The Shepherds' Surprise!	214
A Lost Lamb	312
The Good Shepherd	326

Sickness

Plagues, Plagues, and More Plagues	98
A Good Neighbor	290
Lazarus, Wake Up!	332
Rise Up and Walk!	408

Sisters

Baby Moses	90
Mary and Martha	300
Lazarus, Wake Up!	332

Slaves

Moses Runs Away	94

Soldiers

Moses Runs Away	94
Moses Leads His People	104
Jericho	122
David and Goliath	156
The Centurion's Faith	264
Arrested!	372
The Cross	384
The Darkest Hour	388

Sons

Cain and Abel	44
Noah Builds a Boat	46
Abraham and Isaac	60
A Plea for Help	86
Baby Moses	90
Samson	132
Hannah's Prayer	142
David the King	160
Solomon	164
Born in a Stable	212
Jesus is Baptized	226

Spies

A Plea for Help	86
Twelve Explorers	116

Stars

Abraham Obeys God	56
Wise Men from the East	216

Storms

The Great Flood	50
Jonah and the Big Fish	198
A Frightening Storm	272
Paul's Shipwreck Adventure	420

Strength

Jericho	122
Gideon	128
Samson	132
David and Goliath	156
The Fiery Furnace	190
Jesus Sends a Helper	404

Teaching

Jesus Visits His Father's House	222
Mountaintop Teaching	244
Things to Remember	248
The Story of the Seeds	252
Two Builders	256
The Good Fruit Tree	262
The Mustard Seed	268
"Love Your Enemies"	260
The Greatest in God's Kingdom	296
Mary and Martha	300
A Rich Fool	304
The Big Party	308
A Lost Lamb	312
The Good Shepherd	326
The Servant of All	348

Temple

David the King	160
Solomon	164
Jesus Visits His Father's House	222

Towers

The Tower of Babel	54

Treasures

David the King	160
Solomon	164
Things to Remember	248
A Priceless Treasure	270

Trees

And Things Began to Grow	18
The Serpent's Lie	40
The Good Fruit Tree	262
The Mustard Seed	268
The Holy City	424

Trust

Noah Builds a Boat	46
Abraham Obeys God	56
Jacob's Dream	74
Moses Leads His People	104
Food from Heaven	110
Water in the Desert	112
David and Goliath	156
The Widow at Zarephath	170
An Angel's Visit	204
Thomas Has Doubts	396
Peter's Second Chance	400
Rise Up and Walk!	408

Victories

Jericho	122
Gideon	128
David and Goliath	156

David the King	160		Two Builders	256
The Fiery Furnace	190		Mary and Martha	300
Daniel and the Lions	194		Saul Sees the Light	416
He Lives!	390			
Peter's Second Chance	400		**Women**	
Jesus Sends a Helper	404		God Makes Woman	38
Jesus Is Coming Back!	426		Isaac and Rebekah	64
			Baby Moses	90
Water			Jericho	122
The Sky and Sea	14		Samson	132
Baby Moses	90		Ruth and Naomi	136
Moses Leads His People	104		Hannah's Prayer	142
Water in the Desert	112		The Widow at Zarephath	170
Elijah	168		Queen Esther	182
Jonah and the Big Fish	198		An Angel's Visit	204
Jesus is Baptized	226		Mary Visits Elizabeth	206
The Woman at the Well	278		The Woman at the Well	278
			Mary and Martha	300
Widows			A Widow's Gift	324
Ruth and Naomi	136		Mary's Gift	340
The Widow at Zarephath	170		He Lives!	390
A Widow's Gift	324			
			Worship	
Wilderness			Jacob's Dream	74
Moses Runs Away	94		David	154
Food from Heaven	110		David the King	160
Water in the Desert	112		Solomon	164
Ten Commandments	114		The Fiery Furnace	190
Twelve Explorers	116		Entering Jerusalem	344
Tempted in the Wilderness	230		Jesus Sends a Helper	404
			Rise Up and Walk!	408
Wisdom			The Holy City	424
Samuel	146		Jesus Is Coming Back!	426
Solomon	164			